VICTORIAN
AND
EDWARDIAN SHOPWORKERS

VICTORIAN AND EDWARDIAN SHOPWORKERS

THE STRUGGLE TO OBTAIN
BETTER CONDITIONS
AND A HALF-HOLIDAY

Wilfred B. Whitaker

DAVID & CHARLES
NEWTON ABBOT

To the memory of James and Rosa Emma Long
who took the 'in-law' out of 'parents-in-law'
and made me one of the family

0 7153 6030 2

Set in 11/13pt Plantin
and printed in Great Britain
by W J Holman Limited Dawlish
for David & Charles (Holdings) Limited
South Devon House Newton Abbot Devon

CONTENTS

CHAPTER ONE

SHOP CONDITIONS

Other than Hours, During the Period,
and the Formation of Trade Unions
for Shop-Assistants

I remember being fascinated, as a small boy in Edwardian days, when I stayed with an uncle who had an iron-monger's shop in a north Dorset market town. Often, as the family had meals in the parlour behind the shop, the shop-bell rang or my uncle heard some sound, and up he stood in his place, from which he could peep through a little glass-covered opening in the wall that commanded the shop door, and, calling out 'shop', set off to attend to the customer. If it was market day he might be a long time returning, for he knew all the farmers and business included a leisurely chat about pigs and cattle and grain.

A similar procedure occurred with an uncle who had a watch-maker's business in a nearby town—only there it was, as often as not, my aunt who attended to customers, for she was often in charge of the shop when my uncle cycled round to the big houses in the neighbourhood to wind and adjust the clocks. Sometimes he had an apprentice, but not always. Of the hours of opening and closing I have no memory, but this uncle told me many years later that in 1881, when he was fourteen and apprenticed to a jeweller in Sturminster Newton, the first 5pm closing came on one day a week—probably a Thursday—and to celebrate it he rode on an old-fashioned bicycle to Blandford and took a train to Bournemouth.

Many of the older generation have similar memories or have heard stories of shop life at the end of the last century. These are passed on to younger generations but usually nobody is very sure of the facts. Others base their picture of shop life on novels, such as the experiences of Mr Polly in the shop and the apprentices' dormitory, as described by H. G. Wells in *The History of Mr Polly*. Wells had had actual grim experience of shop life and he dealt with it again in *Kipps*, telling of the hierarchy among the apprentices.

But by itself this is not reliable history. It is a mixture of elaborated or half-forgotten memories and the necessity to tell a good story. We will now try to depict more completely the living and working conditions in the larger London area and provincial houses of business.

The living-in system was general. It was the natural development of the old apprenticeship system where the apprentice was one of the master's family. Equally naturally, once the number of apprentices grew beyond the family limits, and the care of assistants was included, an institutional form of life became necessary and the Victorians were unable to devise institutional living on any but very rigid lines. Human beings—especially youthful ones—in the mass were endowed with evil propensities and these must be eradicated or controlled by strict discipline, which meant a multiplicity of rules. An age which had made a god of work and money was frightened of leisure hours, except for the very wealthy. The very same urge, to spend as little money as possible unless it brought cash dividends—dividends in human happiness did not find much place in the balance sheet—which had led to the crowded, congested industrial areas, led the shop-owner to provide the minimum of space for those he had to house on his premises. Beyond a place to sleep and eat, little was needed. Some owners provided a room in which they put a few books—and called it a library. To most any concession to leisure pursuits was superfluous for there was not meant to be any leisure. Sunday, it is true, was not a working day—so, in many establishments, the inmates were expected to fend for themselves for the greater part of the day being shut out from 10am or thereabouts until 9.0 or 10.0 in the evening. The employers seemed able to close their minds to the problem of how these employees were to spend a wet or cold day or where they were to eat. Although Sunday was for church-going even the most zealous did not spend every hour of the day in church—and they did eat! Even if not shut out from the business house and even if meals were provided, many assistants spent the hours of Sunday walking into the neighbouring countryside—which might mean a long journey—and there was the temptation for the men to spend the evening in the public house. Others, especially the girls and women, were so tired that they spent the greater part of the day in bed. In either case they often incurred the displeasure of the employer who liked his employees to appear in church because it looked more respectable, and that was an essential business requisite.

Edward Flower, writing in 1843 of a house in Liverpool, said that in that business the assistants were not allowed to go out at all except on Sunday. He tells us that, with regard to provision for sleeping at the time, it was usual to put from six to sixteen in a small room, usually two in a bed, although some establishments allowed a bed to each assistant. Significantly he suggested that the mortality rate was very high but this was not realised by the public because when assistants grew pale and sickly they were dismissed and sent home, where they died.[1]

The fact that assistants had no roof, if dismissed, meant that employers could impose almost any conditions they liked.

Employees from a distance often had not the money to get home if they lost their job. Others feared to face the disgrace of return under such conditions and had no idea where to find other employment.

William Ablett, writing in 1854, gave a picture of conditions far removed from the normal life of the drapery worker. Seeking to encourage the industrious apprentice to rise to a position of eminence, with rhetorical splendour he asked: 'Take the drapery trade as it is, where can you see a better?' He claimed: 'It is light and pleasant, and the members of it are well paid.' Where clerks were sometimes unemployed for long periods it was easy to obtain 'comfortable situations' for efficient young drapers. In addition: 'In the drapery trade its members are housed, and their meals are provided with punctuality, and invariably with liberality, so that there is no real occasion to expend one's salary, except for clothing, and that, with economy, is but trifling.'[2]

A book of nearly 250 pages, published in 1853, provided a lot of detailed information to enable a person to start a small shop as a chemist or confectioner or ironmonger etc. The writer suggested that the owner must consider the health and happiness of those he employed and he evidently supported the idea of shorter working hours. He provided his picture of the ideal shopkeeper in these words:

> If we might draw the portrait of a shopkeeper we would paint him thus: a man cheerfully rendering his best labour and knowledge to serve those who approach his counter, and place confidence in his transactions; making himself agreeable alike to rich and poor, but never resorting to mean subterfuge and deception to gain approbation and support. Frugal in his own expenditure, that, in deriving profits from trade, he may not trespass unduly upon the interests of others; but so holding the balance between man and man, that the eye of his soul should discover no bias in the beam to reprove his conscience when the day comes for him to repose from his labours and live upon the fruits of his industry.[3]

In contrast to the description of things as they might be there is Frederick Ross writing in 1854 about the meagre arrangements for the domestic comfort of London shopmen living in. Because they were needed in the shop until late, sitting-rooms for them were often deemed unnecessary. There was no opportunity for social intercourse except the tavern. Often they were dismissed on marriage, 'for it is considered an axiom that a married man is not so effective a salesman as one who is single'. The bedrooms were uncomfortable and often three beds, with two men in each, were placed in one room. Often a man's salary, if he were ill, was stopped and he was expected to leave his bed to go to the dining-room for meals or go without food. On Sunday a man often stayed in bed until noon, unless he had friends to visit or went on a railway excursion. On this last point the writer commented: 'Much as may be urged by well-meaning man on the desecration of the Sabbath by excursion trains, it cannot be denied that the opportunity thus afforded them of escaping from the densely populated city is physically beneficial.'[4]

Although the conditions of women employed as dressmakers or milliners in the workrooms of large shops is strictly outside the subject of shop-assistants, obviously those living on the premises were sharing the same or similar accommodation to those who served behind the counter. The unsatisfactory nature of such conditions in the early 1860s was the subject of an article in the *Social Science Review* in 1864. This said that bedrooms were rarely satisfactory, usually too crowded, often with four in a small room while 'the absence of comfort and even decency which is too commonly found is altogether indefensible'.[5] The provision for washing was defective, there was often no bathroom, frequently there was no sitting-room and meals were taken in the kitchen, or in a room in a basement.

Interesting evidence about the conditions for shop-assistants, and others, living in, which prevailed in the seventies, is provided in a long article that first appeared in the *Church of England Magazine* and was reproduced in the *Wesleyan Methodist Magazine* for February 1873 under the title, 'Philanthropic

Labour in the Metropolis'. It referred to the unhappy lot of young women living in large London business houses where the hours of work were 8am to 8, 9 or 10pm, with no half-holiday. It said that in many cases the assistants were expected to spend Sunday away from the house, and no food was provided. The writer stated:

> For those whose salaries are small, or worse still, for the 'improvers', who have no salary, the Sunday is a dreadful problem . . . Some walk about the streets, some sit in the parks. Some can be traced going from church to church, to find one which is warmed, where they can rest and doze through the time of service before again setting out on their weary pilgrimage. In all weathers these girls may be seen in the cemeteries on Sundays, glad of a place to sit down in . . . In the places to which they resort to buy food, the acquaintances which they must make, and the snares into which they fall, are only the natural result of a state of things which is a disgrace to any Christian country.

In passing one may wonder why the regular worshippers in the churches these girls visited never noticed them, or inquired into their presence. The veneer of respectable church-going often hid a complete indifference to the claims of Christianity for thoughtfulness for, and kindness to, one in need.

The writer exempted most of the larger West End houses from his censure. They provided sitting-rooms and proper food on Sunday. 'But in the East End this is not the case.' Then the article described an interesting experiment which had been started by a lady at 90 Camden Street, Camden Town. At her own expense she had founded and opened a house to provide food, shelter and sympathy for these unfortunate girls. It had been running for three months and was under the direction of a committee of ladies. It was open every day—not just on Sunday —for girls who were out of employment and had no home. Again one may note that it was touching a problem already mentioned, which was to remain without solution for a very long time. Many girls could not benefit from this home, for an employer's reference was needed to become a regular member. Even so it met a real need, for frequently seasonal trade meant the sudden discharge of employees—forty-five in a week by one house, the article says.

The only requirements for becoming a member of this home were set out in this article as

> references to present and preceding employer, a payment of an annual fee of ten shillings and sixpence, or six shillings half yearly. For this the member has the use of reading- and dressing-room at all times; her name is registered without further charge for re-engagements: certainty of a home at moderate charge when seeking a situation, or on Sundays, or if ill; besides such other advantages as the committee hope public liberality will enable them to provide for their protégés. The charge for Sunday, which includes three comfortable meals, is one shilling. For remaining from Saturday till Monday, one shilling and sixpence. For medical attendance and medicine, per visit, one shilling. The rooms are clean, commodious, and orderly. Each bedroom is fitted with three small iron beds, allowing each inmate to have a bed for herself, chest of drawers, etc. The beds have warm blankets, snowy sheets, and counterpanes. It would be impossible to find better or more tempting quarters in the same space; the beds are better than many families in comfortable circumstances can afford.[6]

That even in the West End of London sleeping conditions, in at least one case, were unsatisfactory at a later date is shown by the evidence of a man quoted by Thomas Sutherst in 1884. This man knew 'of an instance in Oxford Street, W., of thirty young ladies who were engaged in the spring of last year, who were obliged to sleep four in a bed, in a room where there was no door, the room being on a level with the young men's sleeping apartment, also having no door'.[7] The cost of a couple of doors —not to say extra beds and rooms—outweighed even Victorian propriety it seems, when the owner could feel reasonably sure that his customers would never know what conditions prevailed behind the scenes.

The phrase 'the customer is always right', invented, one suspects, by some Victorian businessman to disarm suspicion of his own attitude to his customers, was certainly not a maxim given by all employers to their assistants to guide their conduct. Nor was the favourite maxim 'Honesty is the best policy' allowed any weight by many if it was a question of honesty towards the customer. One would not accuse all, or even the majority, of employers of forcing their employees to use dishonest methods of sale but the references to these practices during the period are disquieting. It seems certain that one of the constant strains upon the overworked assistant was the knowledge that he or she would be censured, and in many shops fired, if a customer left a shop without purchasing an article. Reference is made in the early forties to a practice in some shops of what was called 'ticketing' goods. In the window an article was shown at a bargain price. The customer was given an inferior article in the shop, but in the dim light or gas light the difference was not detected. If a customer was suspicious or obstinate enough to demand the article displayed in the window the assistant serving such a customer incurred the employer's displeasure.

In other shops assistants were encouraged to sell damaged or old stock at the same price as up-to-date stock by giving them a premium on all such goods which they sold—and obviously they could not sell them honestly.[8] Such methods led the Rev William Landels, writing in 1856, to say, 'I have it on unquestionable authority that there are masters in London who require their young men to tell lies from morning till night'. He instanced yet another dishonest method of sale, namely several prices for one article, known only to the assistant, who was expected to decide the one the particular customer was likely to pay. Landels emphasised that these practices were followed by professedly Christian employers and that as a result 'men who seek the highest interest of these young men have become tired of recommending them to professors of religion, because in many circumstances their influence has driven those who were religiously disposed into practical or avowed infidelity'.[9] These statements came in a public lecture, which was later printed on behalf of the Early Closing Association, and cannot be dismissed as the wild surmises of a disgruntled parson; for the association was a body of influential employers who, while presumably not countenancing the wrongs condemned, knew the methods used by many of their fellows or they would not have sanctioned such statements going out with their support.

John Hollingshead, in a book published in 1861, referred to the formation of an 'Association for Suppressing the Practice of Falsely Labelling Goods for Sale'. The group consisted of manufacturers and traders who aimed to prevent open fraud—the need for which the writer illustrates as follows:

> The British merchant has been found guilty of selling pieces of calico, nominally thirty-six yards in length, never measuring more than thirty yards. He is found guilty of selling thirty-six inches of silk lace, and calling it fifty-four inches; of selling grosses of tapes containing only sixty yards, as if they represented the full quantity of one hundred and forty-four yards ... He is found guilty of increasing the weight of the hogshead, compared with the sugar it contains, from twelve per cent of the gross weight to seventeen per cent. He is found guilty of pirating designs, of imitating the wrappers of well-known makers, and of forging popular trade marks. He is found guilty of selling ribbons in long lengths, the first three yards of which (being the part usually unrolled) are of a quality infinitely superior to the bulk of the piece. He is found guilty of reducing the weight of candles (sold in bunches) until the buyer is defrauded of two ounces in his pound. He is guilty of mixing cotton with silk, and adulterating cloth. In proportion as this adulteration increases, the labels become more prominent in asserting the purity of the articles; and 'All Wool' or 'All Silk' are printed in the largest of golden letters, on the purest of cream-coloured cards ... These frauds are all considered, by those who practise and grow rich on them, as allowable customs of the trade.[10]

If even a few of the manufacturers and merchants acted so, it is not surprising that too often the small shopkeeper was none too scrupulous. It is characteristic, too, of the period, that the writer made sarcastic comment that the new society did not propose to use the law against offenders but only the persuasion of gentle remonstration.

Much more serious frauds were carried out in the food sold to the public. The *Lancet*, in 1851, conducted an inquiry into the 'present condition of various articles of diet', and its report said, 'It is now ascertained beyond the possibility of a doubt, that frauds are committed to an enormous extent, and that the public health is imperilled by the most profligate adulterations of human food'. It was found that coffee was adulterated by chicory, roasted corn, beans, potato and burnt sugar.

Brown sugar contained so many impurities that the *Lancet* said, 'the brown sugars of commerce are, in general, in a state wholly unfit for human consumption'. Arrowroot was found to be adulterated with sago-meal and potato-flour so that 'the public is extensively defrauded of its money, and the revenue of its income'. Pepper and mustard were often so impure that, in the case of the latter, whatever price was paid it could 'scarcely ever be obtained' in a genuine form. Bread was often underweight and adulterated with alum. Oatmeal often had barley meal mixed with it. (Workhouses usually economised by buying adulterated oatmeal.)

The investigation found that black teas were usually genuine but green tea, except from Assam, was often glazed with coloured matter and so likely to be injurious. Used tea-leaves were often made up with gum etc and re-sold as black tea or fabricated with leaves other than those of tea. It is not surprising that it found milk was often 10 to 50 per cent water.[11]

The *Lancet* had been founded in 1823 by Thomas Wakley and this investigation, which he instigated, led to some improvement in the standard of drugs and food but, even after the Adulteration Act of 1860, Wakley was not very satisfied with the resulting conditions. A recent writer has pointed out that in the factory areas of the country in early Victorian times, the small shopkeeper had every temptation to sell adulterated goods and to use incorrect scales.[12] It is reasonably safe to assume that this was not unknown at the end of the century.

To turn to another aspect of life and conditions for shop-workers it can be shown that in many small shops the lack of toilet facilities was a hardship. Adolph Smith, FCS, in evidence before a Parliamentary Committee in 1892, stated that in many shops there was no sanitary convenience and no opportunity to obtain even a glass of water. As a result the assistants had to run out to the nearest public house to get a drink or to relieve themselves. He suggested that here was a matter which the temperance societies might well investigate. His evidence is also a reminder that, at the end of the century, an abuse of the living-in system which still remained was that in some premises men were turned out at 10.30 on Sunday morning and not allowed to return until night.[13]

In 1896 Will Anderson, who appears to have been a commercial traveller but who had been a grocer's assistant, published a cardboard-covered little book of 110 pages called *The Counter Exposed,* which tells us a great deal of what he had experienced and seen as an apprentice and assistant. His first position on finishing his apprenticeship was with a grocery firm, having about a dozen employees, somewhere in Kent. Internal evidence suggests either Rochester or Gillingham, but Anderson names no town. He lived in, and started work at 7 o'clock having already had breakfast. There was the usual short break for dinner—in this case only twenty-five minutes—and a twenty minute break for tea. The total weekly hours were 85-90. Most of his companions were under twenty-one years old; two were under sixteen and he thinks one was under fourteen. He makes this revealing comment:

> I take credit to myself for having made the Sundays a little more wholesome by inducing some of the employees to ramble with me through Cobham and Upnor, or over the hills into Gravesend—dicing and drinking in the bedroom had formerly been the order of the day—but it is a feeble sort of credit, all our recreations

B

were fouled with excess; the stupor resulting from long hours and overwork sought to recover itself in satiety.

Later he worked in a Lancashire town for a large firm of wholesale and retail grocers employing about forty men. Here he lived away from the business but as no tea break was allowed except on Fridays and Saturdays, when closing hours were 10pm and 11pm, it was usually 8pm before he reached home for tea, having had no food since mid-day. As only half an hour was allowed for dinner that meal was usually 'a seven or ten minutes' scramble at the nearest restaurant for the least indigestible viands. He adds, 'My means only just allowed of my renting part of a cellar-kitchen at a long distance from the shop, for which I paid 12s 6d per week, breakfast and tea inclusive'. Such conditions must have been typical of thousands who lived away from their place of business. At the end of a month of these conditions, aggravated by an employer who was 'the most incorrigible monster it has been my lot to have business relations with' who terrorised his employees, Anderson had a nervous breakdown. Anderson says that a qualified assistant earned about 18s a week at the minimum and in exceptional cases after about ten years' service might reach a maximum of 35s a week.[14]

Two years after Anderson's book, the *Daily Chronicle* published a number of articles on shop conditions contributed by one of its staff who had been detailed to investigate the situation. These show that bad living-in conditions, the tyrannical shop-walker, the rushed meals and irksome rules were all too common features of life for a large number of assistants. One article pointed out that many shops would not engage an assistant unless she had a home or friends to go to on Sundays because, as one firm put it, 'we like the house to ourselves on Sunday'. The picture is not all black. The correspondent was taken over a large establishment in south London where there were well-ventilated dormitories, good bath-rooms, cheerful sitting-rooms and a library, and where the food was good. Even so there was the air of institutionalism. No pictures could be put on bedroom walls and each room had three or four inmates. A point so often made earlier in the century was noted, namely that many employers would not engage married men. In some cases an assistant did marry and continued to live in through the week and spent Sunday with his wife, but as soon as this fact was discovered he was dismissed.

There are many references to the numerous and often trivial rules, which carried severe penalties for a breach. The Women's Industrial Council had employed Miss Margaret Bondfield to investigate conditions in shops for them, and the *Daily Chronicle* writer quoted from the result of this investigation as well as from his own inquiries. In one case the rules included these: that the house closed at 11pm or on Saturdays at 12pm and that the gas was turned out fifteen minutes later, after which anyone showing any light would be dismissed; that bedrooms on Sunday must be cleared by 10.20am and not re-entered until 12.30pm; that no pictures must be put on the walls; that no assistant must enter any bedroom but her own; that if anyone was ill the fact must be reported before 9am to the housekeeper, and the house doctor, for whose services sixpence a month was deducted from wages, would be called if necessary—no other doctor was allowed to enter the house; that no hot water was obtainable on Saturday or Sunday nights; and that no flowers were to be put in water glasses or bottles.

In another place any assistant who was ill had to remain in the ordinary room, shared by others, and had to go home if she had not recovered in a week. A shop in Holloway had seventy-five rules for the assistants in the shop: they could be fined three-pence for 'gossiping, standing in groups, or lounging about in an unbusinesslike manner'; a similar amount for bringing a newspaper into the shop, or for omitting to replace paper, string etc in its allotted place, or for omitting the date on a bill. The fine was sixpence for cutting material in such a way as to leave an unsaleable length. If an assistant allowed a customer to go out without making a purchase he or she was reported, unless the shop-walker had been called. In the latter case one can imagine that there would later be trouble for the assistant. A firm in Westbourne Grove, London, had 198 rules and Whiteley's, Queensway, 159. One West End firm imposed a fine of 5s for losing a duplicate bill and one girl had had to pay this when the value of the bill was threepence.

The practice of the 'premium' (paid for selling inferior quality goods, which prevailed as we have seen in the mid-century) still continued. In many shops each assistant knew that he or she was expected to sell goods to a certain amount in the week—this amount was called the 'book'—and there was trouble if the sum were not reached.

The food provided for the assistants living-in was often monotonous, even when wholesome. An Islington shop had followed this menu for years for dinner: Sunday, pork; Monday, hot beef; Tuesday, cold beef; Wednesday, hot mutton; Thursday, cold mutton; Friday, hot beef; Saturday, cold beef. The menu of an East End drapery establishment was given in greater detail. Breakfast was always bread, with butter or dripping, and tea or coffee. Dinner was: Monday, hot roast mutton and potatoes; Tuesday, cold beef, potatoes and currant pudding; Wednesday, stew; Thursday, cold salt beef and potatoes; Friday, hot roast beef, potatoes and boiled pudding; Saturday, cold beef, potatoes and bread and butter pudding. Bread was supplied every day and ale and water. For tea there was bread, butter and tea each day. Supper consisted of bread, cheese, butter, ale and water, and about twice a week a pudding. Many houses fined an assistant who left food on his or her plate. At the Clapham firm of Arding and Hobbs an assistant had been dismissed for refusing to pay a 5s fine for leaving meat on his plate and the firm had dismissed with him a brother who had only been apprenticed three days with them.[15]

Many will wonder that the assistants accepted these conditions —petty regulations, unsatisfactory living conditions, long hours —so unprotestingly. This is to forget the apathy of the assistants from the early days, and many factors contributed to this attitude. Some of these will be clear as we look at the efforts which were made to form a trade union for the shopworkers.

In 1888 a writer said: 'Years of submission to unjust laws and cruelty have infused into assistants a cowardly fear, the immediate result of which is that there are hundreds of assistants who dare not sign a petition in favour of reform, however trifling, if their employers entertain opposite opinions.' He went on to claim that the first and greatest need, if reform were to be secured, was the combination of shop-assistants, and he put second to this the need to change the system whereby an employer could hold the threat of refusing a reference over the head of an employee, and the need to secure better food and accommodation for those living in.[16]

Only occasionally did the assistants show a spirited action. One instance was in February 1891 when the refusal of certain tradesmen in the Westminster Bridge Road, London, to join the early closing movement led forty assistants to march up and down outside the premises of one of these, a boot-shop distributing bills which read, 'Don't shop at Frith's'. Two were summoned for obstruction and bound over. But apparently the protest was not without some result for almost immediately it was announced that Messrs Frith had agreed to re-adopt the 2pm closing on Thursday at their Clapham Junction branch.[17]

In March 1891 the National Union of Shop-Assistants was formed at a conference held in Birmingham to which representatives went from Manchester, Liverpool, London, Sunderland, Leeds, Hull, Birmingham, Bolton, Oldham, Ashton and South Wales. In almost all cases these representatives came from groups of assistants who had left, or broken away from, local early closing associations because they felt that the latter were achieving little or nothing. The earliest of these groups seems to have been formed in Manchester in the latter part of 1889. By 1891 this group tried to run a weekly journal called *Shop Life Reform* which sold at 1d a copy, but after seven months the venture had to be ended. In its first number, it gave an account of a meeting of the Manchester Salford and District Grocers' Association which carried a resolution supporting efforts to secure a compulsory half-holiday. One speaker said that if there was no act, they would soon have only poor assistants. The same kind of thing was tried in Bolton where a penny paper, called the *Leader*, was started in 1890 and gave news of the Shop-Assistants' Association, while a rival journal was called the *Labour Light and Local Trades Union Journal*, which gave information about the same association and about the Liverpool and District Hairdressers' Union, which was presumably run by longer established unions belonging to other trades.[18]

The chief office of the National Union of Shop-Assistants was in Manchester and its secretary was Mr William Johnson. By 1892 branches had been started at Salford, Cardiff, Swansea, Llanelly, Aberdare, Newcastle, Middlesbrough, Jarrow, Blythe, Barnsley- and Crewe, in addition to the places which had sent representatives to the first meeting in 1891. Mr Johnson, in evidence before the select committee on the Shop Hours' Bill in 1892, gave the membership as 3,500 and the objects of the union as to reduce the hours of work and secure adequate wages. He said that he thought fifty working hours should be the maximum, saying that if the co-operative shops managed with forty-eight hours, private traders ought to be able to do so. He suggested that shops should open from 9am to 7pm on five days a week, with an hour allowed for dinner and half an hour for tea, and that closing time on Saturday should be 1pm. He pointed out that his union considered that a uniform closing hour for all trades was necessary in each place and he instanced the fact that in Manchester Messrs Lewis's had retarded the half-holiday movement because they were a multiple store which refused to close early when grocers, boot and tailoring shops were prepared to do so. 'This particular firm obstructs the passage of any reduction of hours for any particular trade with which it is connected, because they will not observe it.'[19]

The need for the union to do something about wages as well as hours is well brought out by another witness before the same committee. Mr Adolph Smith, FCS, said: 'Even the docker, over whom so much sympathy was expended, is in some respects better off than the shop-assistant. Quite a chorus of shop-assistants acclaimed in our presence that they wished they could get "the docker's tanner". The Blue Book Report on the Shop Hours' Regulation Bill establishes that shop-assistants are generally worked 85 hours a week, and this at 6d an hour would equal £2 2s 6d a week, but they rarely receive anything like so large a salary.' He pointed out, too, that a mechanic who worked forty-eight to fifty-four hours a week was paid eightpence or more an hour.[20]

The National Union of Shop-Assistants had been preceded in 1889 by a London association called the United Shop-Assistants' Union with similar aims.[21] Thus there were stirrings which indicated that a minority of assistants were seeking for a more realistic approach to their problems than offered by the early closing associations.

In 1898 Miss Margaret Bondfield, who was to become in 1929 the first woman to be a cabinet minister, became assistant secretary of the National Union of Shop-Assistants. For two years, at the instigation of the Women's Industrial Council, she had been investigating the conditions under which shop-assistants worked. She writes of her experience as follows:

> In industrial districts shops were open until 9 o'clock on Fridays and any time from 10 o'clock to midnight on Saturdays. At a shop in Kilburn I remember the employer took a census of the amount of money taken after 8 o'clock and declared it did not pay for the gas; but he dared not shut up earlier than his competitors for fear he should lose a customer to them. At a small shop in Commercial Road my employer would send me out to scout around and see if the shops over the way showed any signs of closing; if they did, we too would hastily and gladly put up the shutters.

While so engaged Miss Bondfield belonged to the union and

she writes that Sunday was the only day when executive meetings of the union could be held, for members had to travel long distances in many cases, travelling by night trains to arrive early on Sunday and leaving again on Sunday night in order to be at business by 7.30 or 8am on Monday.[22]

By 1898 the union had eighty-six branches and a membership of 3,286, yet, as it calculated that there were 1,750 towns and cities in the United Kingdom, each of which ought to have a branch if the union was really to be effective, its influence could not be very great.[23]

The year before, the writer of a Fabian tract, *Shop Life and its Reform*, had stressed the need for shop-assistants to unite in their own defence and had given some of the reasons why it was so difficult to induce them to do so. In his opinion, 'with the doubtful exception of the victim of the sweated home industries, no other class of workers have shown themselves so careless of their responsibilities towards themselves and their fellows as the shop-assistants'. He considered that 'a factory-owner who ventured to treat a single cotton operative with a fraction of the tyranny which is the prerogative of any shopkeeper would soon raise a storm about his ears'. He listed the reasons why it was so difficult to organise the shop-assistants: first, they were a nomadic class; second, they had not much time in which to hold meetings; third, the economic pressure of young people crowding into the trade; fourth, 'Social status, not economic law, is the ruin alike of shop-assistants and clerks. Very many of them are prevented by their sham gentility from helping in the organisation of their class.' The fifth reason the writer gave was that they had a half-conscious feeling that one day they would become employers themselves.[24] The writer could have added that as so many assistants were only in their teens they were hardly able to understand the need for co-operation. Together with this was the fact that many dare not risk dismissal, which would often be the consequence of even a suggestion of union membership. Especially was this so among men in their thirties or forties, who could have furnished experienced leadership, for a male draper after the age of thirty-five had very little chance of securing a new situation.

The apathy of the average assistant was attacked by Will Anderson whose book has already provided material for this chapter. He writes that two and a half centuries before, 'at the cry of Apprentices and Clubs, the youth of London rallied to each other's assistance; now they are tamely content to have employment at any price, and by a brief parole of about $1\frac{1}{2}$ hours per night are cozened into acquiescence with their lot'. Later he comments, 'much today is expected from a spread of education to the masses, and much may result properly directed, but here is a class that has enjoyed all the advantages of a liberal training, but has less independence and solidarity than mechanics'. He adds that he is not disparaging education but paying a tribute to the efficacy of trade unionism.

Anderson brings out another of the obstacles to fostering a desire for trade union action in the shop-assistant when he writes :

> And remember it is his 'apartness' that is at the bottom of half his grievances, as illustrated in the disaffection that exists in his own ranks, and the 'caste' amongst the different trades in which he is engaged. The draper's assistant affects a certain superiority over the grocer's assistant, the grocer's assistant has his own idea about the draper's assistant, the ironmonger's assistant is criticised by both, and in his turn is alive to the merits of his own position, whilst the chemist's assistant looks down on all or tries not to, and the banker's clerk will no doubt feel a little disgust at my having alluded at all to him.[25]

The writer of the *Daily Chronicle* articles of 1898 refers to the poor support given by the assistants to their two trade unions. In spite of the efforts of Sir John Lubbock and all the voluntary work to improve conditions little had been achieved, he felt, and he concluded that 'in the main the shop-assistants remain a forgotten and negligible class, living a hard and dreary and unhealthy life, a sacrifice to their own notions of self-respect and the throng of thoughtless purchasers to whom they are often less than nothing'.[26]

In April 1906 there was set up a committee, under the chairmanship of the Right Hon Thomas Shaw MP, the Lord Advocate for Scotland, to inquire into the working of the Truck System of wages. It sat for over two and a half years and in its report, presented to Parliament, there is a mass of evidence with reference to the living-in conditions of shop-assistants. This shows quite clearly that the new century had seen little improvement in conditions. Once again, in reading what was stated by those who had experienced shop conditions in the previous twenty years, one is amazed that the picture they gave has been ignored by almost all who consider the social life of late Victorian and early Edwardian England.

Miss Margaret Bondfield told the committee of her own experiences as a young assistant in a shop:

> When I was a young apprentice myself, I was employed in a house at Brighton; for the purpose of sleeping the assistants, they took various houses in back streets. The house that I was put to sleep in was No 1 ——— Street. My sleeping-room was on the ground floor, with the window facing on to the street, so that one could step into the street from the window and back into the room from the street, without going through the door at all. I was put into a room with a woman of mature age who had a life of a most undesirable kind; that was my first experience of a living-in house.[27]

So much for the vaunted protection for young girls which the living-in- system claimed to provide! It is worth putting with this the experience of Mr Frank Tilley, a draper in business for himself when he gave evidence, who describes how in 1897 he was one of ten assistants, male and female, in a provincial town, who were housed in a private building under the care of a deaf labourer and his wife. Both sexes used one staircase on to which all the rooms opened and, as he puts it, there was every opportunity for immorality. He adds that the assistants conducted themselves with self-respect—a credit to them, but the system was a reflection upon the employer.[28]

Miss Bondfield described the room she occupied on another occasion when one of 400 employees. She and three others had a room measuring 2,662 cubic feet, on the fourth floor. The fireplace was boarded up, and each person had a bed, a chest of drawers, a washstand, a looking-glass; there was a strip of carpet, one or two wooden chairs and Venetian blinds but no curtains to the window. She makes no mention of a bathroom and later, when questioned by the committee about washing arrangements in general where assistants live in, she states that bathrooms are exceptional and, where provided, inadequate, saying 'many girls do not like to wash themselves all over in the presence of their room mates; they wash their face and neck; they sometimes do not even wash their feet; one reason why they do not wash their feet is very frequently because there is not a sufficient supply of water in the room. But apart from that, there is that natural shrinking against exposing their naked persons in rooms with people they know little about.'

In another establishment, described by Miss Bondfield, rooms had been divided by half partitions with two-foot spaces at the top and six-inch spaces at the bottom. On one floor fourteen 'rooms' so provided had no windows; ventilation was supposed to come over the top of the partitions from a sick room at the end which had three windows in it which were never opened. In each of these rooms or sections there were two, three or four beds and there was no space for any other furniture. 'The wash-basins are fixed up on shelves, and in the section containing three beds there is not enough floor space to enable the three girls to dress at the same time. Two have to wait in bed until one has cleared out of the room.' All clothing had to be kept in cupboards in the corridors. There was no privacy, and conversation could be heard from one section to the other.

Over and over again Miss Bondfield and others give examples of crowded, badly ventilated, insanitary conditions where the danger if fire broke out was tremendous. One is not surprised to read that Miss Bondfield told the committee that one group of assistants complained that, 'The beds were infested with bugs which could only be subdued by a lavish use of Keatings' powder, administered by the assistants at their own expense'.

At another house Miss Bondfield reported that an outbreak of typhoid fever in 1899 had meant six deaths in fifty-four cases, and the cause of the outbreak was traced to defective drainage infecting the water supply.

Miss Bondfield suggested that many employers kept the living-in system because they could then use their assistants for extra long hours. In a properly run shop this was not done but where an owner was trying to cut down staff he could get the work of tidying up, window-dressing etc done at a late hour at night with staff who lived in.[29] It is interesting that Mr A. E. Derry, a partner of Derry and Toms in Kensington High Street, with 260 women living in, told the committee that the firm could not afford to give up the living-in system because the premises they now used for their purpose would be useless, the employees would require extra pay if they lived out, and the profit made on feeding them would be lost. Yet he said that he was not in favour of the system. It is also interesting to find that he told the committee that he knew of establishments where assistants were turned out on Sunday and no food provided for them.[30]

Mr Ernest Debenham, of Debenhams Ltd of Wigmore Street and the City, was opposed to living in, and told the committee how his firm had reduced the number so doing from 366 out of 460 in 1893 to 44 out of 676 in 1907.[31] Mr Richard Burbidge of Harrods Ltd, employing over 4,000 people, did not have living in but provided dinner and tea on the premises. He said that the average wage for a woman of twenty-two would be 23s a week with an average commission of 6s 6d if she had meals at the shop; and 28s and the 6s 6d commission if she took her meals elsewhere. A man of twenty-five would average 30s a week with an average commission of 8s together with dinner and tea free.[32]

Miss Margaret Oliver, an assistant, favoured living in and would not live out. She was one of 200 employees, whose firm was not disclosed to the public, in a place where conditions and food were good. The protection which living in provided for girls and the difficulty of securing her own accommodation were her reasons for upholding the system.[33]

A woman of twenty-six employed in a draper's shop at Bradford, whose name was not disclosed because she feared to lose her job, gave evidence of living-in conditions among some 120 asistants. Later the employer, Mr Rendell, proved to be a very shifty witness before the committee but, by dint of questioning, had to admit the truth of at any rate some of the points made by his assistant. She described how fifteen women were distributed on two floors as follows: four in one room, one in one, two in one, two in another, three in one, three in another. There was a bed, looking-glass and chair for each person. They all had to wash in a room set aside for the purpose which had no bath but four basins of which, at the time, only one could be used. One was apparently permanently unusable and two had been choked up for a fortnight. In the same room was the only convenience. If anyone wanted hot water she had to fetch it up two flights of stairs in a receptacle she had bought herself. Each made her own bed and one clean sheet a fortnight was provided. The wages were £35 a year and one shilling a week of this had to be paid for personal laundry which the shop sent out and which the witness reported was done satisfactorily. The committee found out from Mr Rendell that the amount allowed for the shilling was 'Two pairs of stockings, six handkerchiefs, six collars, a night-shirt, knickers and chemises'. The menu for meals was, according to the woman witness, for breakfast, bread, 'margarine butter', and coffee; dinner, beef or mutton or ham, pudding and tart, and on some days two spoonfuls of soup; tea, bread, butter, tea; supper, bread, cheese, coffee. She said the meat was often tainted—the employer had been brought to court in 1898 and fined for providing meat unfit for human food, but on appeal the decision had been reversed because the meat had not been exposed for sale—the milk in the tea often sour, the cheese uneatable and there was often no milk for the coffee. On Sunday, she said, dinner was better and cake was provided at tea-time; this, at any rate, was not a place where the assistants were turned out on Sunday.[34] That such places were still to be found is shown clearly in the evidence of other witnesses before the committee, as for example one London shop, employing twelve assistants, whose owner told the witness (a new arrival from Cardiff) that she must be out of the house between 10am and 10pm on Sundays and advised her to go to the YWCA.[35]

Mr J. A. Seddon MP emphasised the injury to health of living-in conditions in many premises—a fact which must be obvious from the evidence we have examined. He reminded the committee that in 1893 Dr Bowrie had told a committee of the House of Lords that 38 per cent of shop-assistants suffered from consumption and that more recently Mr Crossley MP had started a sanatorium in Cheshire at which, he had said, half the patients suffering from consumption were shop girls.[36]

Mr P. C. Hoffman, on being asked by the committee to account for the small proportion of assistants in a union—probably 22,000 in the National Union of Shop-Assistants out of some half a million assistants who could have joined—said 'In the first place, a large number of assistants have in years gone by hoped to be in business upon their own account; they have considered themselves to be superior to the ordinary worker, and it is only as businesses are growing up larger and larger and the distributive trades are becoming more highly organised that they are beginning to understand that they are a permanent wage-earning class'.

When he was asked what happened to men over thirty-five or forty who had been shop-assistants—for witnesses agreed that there were few men in the trade as ordinary assistants over thirty-five—he said, 'they simply sort of slide out into all sorts of branches—insurance agents, booksellers, and things of that kind'. In South Wales, many became miners.[37]

Alongside bad living-in conditions and long hours of work, still went, in some shops, the dishonest methods of trading and the pressure on assistants to use these methods—as is illustrated in a book called *Sweated Industry and the Minimum Wage*, published in 1907 by Clementine Black. She describes the old system of premiums—certain goods to be pushed by the assistant who obtained a small commission on sale—as still in use, saying that in some shops an assistant had to press two such articles on every customer. She said there were still shops where a girl was instantly dismissed if she did not effect a sale. Some customers were annoyed that goods they did not want were pressed on them, but she commented: 'Such customers are apt to forget the great commercial truth that shops exist not to supply the needs of the public but to fill the pockets of the shopkeeper.' She quotes, too, a provincial draper as telling an assistant, 'Anyone can sell people what they want. Remember that I keep you to sell people what they don't want.'[38] Truly the lot of a shop-assistant in many cases was far from being a happy one even in the prosperous times of Edward VII.

If the conditions for the shop-assistant had changed but little, the appearance of the shops and the attractiveness of their displays had altered very much. In the City of London by the 1850s plate glass began to be used to replace small panes of ordinary glass and window-dressing became more skilled and artistic. A writer in 1859 describes the scene in Regent Street at mid-day in summer as follows:

> The shops are as brilliant as they may be. How richly falls the drapery of those emblazoned shawls through the fair plate-glass. How the rows of 'loves of bonnets', each upon its peg, gladden and sadden at the same moment the bright female eyes. How chastely luscious in its artistic network depend the rich clusters of precious old-fashioned lace. How gorgeously shines the plate—massive lumps of chased and carved and graven and frosted silver and gold; and how pleasant to look upon be the tempting cakes, and bons-bons, and jellies, ranged round the glistening barley-sugar cages in the confectioner's window.[39]

A cartoon in *Punch* in 1860 shows a large shop-window divided into domed panels of large sheets of glass behind which are displayed a few ladies' hats on stands. There is no suggestion of crowding the articles on show.[40]

An article in *Chambers's Journal* in 1864 deals with London shop-fronts and says:

> They form one of the most prominent indications of the grandeur and wealth of the metropolis. Enormous plate-glass windows, gilded or polished brass frames, expensive mirrors, polished mahogany frame, and all sorts of fancy woodwork; sometimes crystal columns, and generally a singular covering of iron Venetian blinds, which roll up and down by intricate machinery, like a stage curtain displaying or concealing the gorgeous scenery within—these are the necessary decorations of a fashionable London shop in the middle of the nineteenth century.[41]

A writer in 1861, in a chapter on shop-windows, has the following amusing description which can be compared with today's notices that, owing to the falling in of the lease, the stock must be sold at give-away prices or that bargain prices are due to the loss of an export order. He says:

> But it is to 'bankrupts' stocks' that women 'most do congregate'. The taste ladies have for 'fifty per cent under prime cost' is extraordinary. There is one shop in St Paul's Churchyard that, with laudable gallantry, make a 'frightful sacrifice' of itself every autumn for their especial pleasure. For a few days previously it puts its shutters up, and retires into itself to contemplate the great act of devotion it is about to perform.
>
> Then, at an appointed time, the shutters are withdrawn, and the mental agony the stock has endured at the thought of its approaching dissolution, is observable. The ribbons lie dishevelled in every corner, the 5,000 dozens of muslins precipitately pitch themselves into the window, as though in despair at not being able to get rid of themselves before the wet weather sets in; lace visites implore you by their emphatic tickets to save them from the wreck; and the glossy satins coax to be removed from the vulgar neighbourhood of 'warranted washing colours'.[42]

Writing about shop-windows in the 1880s Lady Violet Greville says :

> Let us first pause before a draper's shop, one of those huge palaces of which the owners rapidly become merchant princes and aspire to alliance with the aristocracy. Who wears all the marvellous sheeney silks and artistic stamped velvets and damasks; who wrap themselves in the glossy furs and soft sealskins, the fashion whereof changeth every season, and weareth out according to the feat of the dressmaker? One year everyone is furred up to the nose until women look more like mummies than charmers, the next year the very tightest and airiest of costumes alone are admissible, with kid bodies and closely clinging jerseys, producing, when used in light colours, much the same effect as Eve's primitive attire.

The writer exclaims at the wealth of England where there is a demand

> for the numberless lace trifles, gaudy ribbons, satins, delicate frills and confections and headdresses, and whatever all the names may be of the various articles that sparkle and dangle and shine and attract in the plate-glass squares that make the delight of ladies' eyes![43]

Before 1850 there were departmental stores such as Bainbridge's of Newcastle or Kendal Milne of Manchester, but from the middle of the century Thomas Wallis in Holborn, Nicholson's in St Paul's Churchyard, Peter Robinson in Oxford Street, London, were expanding, soon to be followed by Derry and Toms in Kensington, John Lewis in Oxford Street and others, which were to become household names. Thus the appearance of the main shopping areas of the big cities was changing all through the second half of the nineteenth century.[44]

This change was increased as gas lighting became more general and more and more of the big shops followed the example of George Hitchcock, in St Paul's Churchyard, who arranged lamps outside the shop to light, by means of reflectors, the window displays. Before the century ended electricity was supplanting gas for lighting.

c

An article by Lady Jeune, in the *Fortnightly Review* for January 1895, contrasted shopping in the West End of London then with a quarter of a century before. She said that twenty-five years earlier, 'an afternoon's shopping was a solemn and dreary affair, when one was received at the door of the shop by a solemn gentleman in black, who in due time delivered one over to another solemn gentleman, and perhaps again to a third, who found one a chair, and in a sepulchral tone of voice uttered some magic words, such as "Silk, Mr Smith", or "Velvet, Mr A", and then departed to seek another victim'. Today, she found that in the stores, 'We are not able to stand against the overwhelming temptations to buy which besiege us at every turn'.[45]

Lady Jeune is glad that the proportion of women assistants to men has increased in the period she is surveying because women are quicker and more understanding than men, and she comments on the patience of the women assistants, apparently not realising that the retention of their job depended on their civility under whatever stress. She does, however, make the comment that 'anyone who has shopped in less fashionable localities, however blunted their powers of observation, must have, over and over again, experienced a feeling of pity for the shop-girl who attends to them. How often has one seen a thin, pallid, anaemic girl behind the counter, hurrying here and there, full of resource, of quickness, of anxiety to please, working from morning to night, without knowing that she is no more fit to be doing such work than she is to draw a cart.'[46] The writer says that hours for shop-assistants are too long, especially in the poorer shops, that generally assistants are discouraged from sitting down, and that more light and ventilation are needed in the shops. Yet she joins her voice to the melancholy chorus decrying a legal remedy for abuses by stating, 'Any legislative interference with the conditions of the working women of England must be done slowly and quietly, for any limitation of the hours of labour as affecting women would only put them at a disadvantage with men'.[47]

Annie Deacock, born in 1863, gives a vivid picture of life in a small, busy family shop in her girlhood. Her father was a successful dairyman and his shop, in Leather Lane, High Holborn, sold not only milk, eggs and butter, but bread. The shop opened at 7.15am and seldom closed before ten or eleven at night while it was often after midnight on Saturdays. Annie says that 'Foodstuffs were not very carefully treated from the standpoint of hygiene. Butter, for instance, would be wrapped in any old scraps of paper. We used to buy up children's copy-books for the purpose, although newspapers were taboo except for outside wrapping. As a refinement of this we gave away little wooden dishes with a pound of butter, and packed it into them for the customer to carry away.' She says that her father supplied eggs to Italian ice-cream merchants who paid their accounts in coppers. Her father did not use a bank but left the money in an iron chest screwed to the floor under the shop counter and often had up to £100 in coppers in it. She says Gamages used the same system, while her uncle, a tobacconist on the corner of Regent Street and Oxford Street, kept all his money under his bed. When the family moved to live at Hornsey in 1879 two of Annie's brothers continued to live at the shop in Leather Lane and the father travelled in daily, getting home late each night, and not much before midnight on Saturdays.[48] Such men, ready to work long hours themselves, saw nothing wrong in expecting assistants to do the same.

CHAPTER TWO

THE START OF THE
EARLY CLOSING ASSOCIATION

Early in the 1840s Liverpool, no less than its neighbour, Manchester, was excited by the agitation of the Chartists and the propaganda of the Anti-Corn Law League. Not far away, in Rochdale, some working men were planning what was to become, in 1844, the first successful co-operative shop. In 1842 not only did the Afghan War end but Hong Kong passed into British hands—signs of the growing pains and material prizes of Empire. The penny post, at the beginning of the decade, heralded swifter and cheaper communications for men of business as well as private correspondents. The country was on the eve of a railway mania and Edwin Chadwick was reporting on the evil sanitary conditions of English towns. At such a time, and in spite of the new handicap—re-imposed after a lapse of over a quarter of a century—of income tax, fixed at 7d in the £ on incomes over £150, a Liverpool shop-assistant, Edward Flower, set up his own business as a draper.

It was a bad time for retail tradesmen yet Flower's action was not unique. What distinguishes him from others who so ventured is that when he became a shopkeeper in 1844, he was the energetic president of an association of drapers' assistants which had been formed six years before to work for a reduction of hours for their kind, and so valuable was his work considered that he was retained in office although, by rule, the association was restricted to assistants.

In 1838 the drapers' assistants had appealed, through the press, to their employers for a reduction in hours which, according to one journal, totalled sixteen a day. This magazine, supporting their case, expressed the hope that ladies would patronise only those shops whose owners accepted the suggested shorter hours.[1]

Edward Flower, in the knowledge gained by the first few years spent with his fellow assistants in trying to achieve their aim by these methods, published in 1843 a book entitled *Hours of Business*. This book reveals an aspect of working life that rarely receives even passing comment in histories of the period written today. It is a small book, few copies of which now exist, for the catalogue of the Library of the British Museum does not list it, with the typically Victorian additional title, 'A glance at the Present System of Business among Shopkeepers and the Effect of that system upon the Young Men Engaged in that Trade, as well as upon Society at Large'. At the beginning the author is prophetic when he expresses himself puzzled that, 'among the philanthropists of this most philanthropic age' who have improved conditions 'of our fellow-creatures without regard to nation, to colour, or to creed', little or no attention has been given to shop-assistants with whom the public have daily contact.[2] A writer at the end of the Victorian era could have said the same!

Although puzzled, Flower ventures one shrewd reason for this state of affairs, namely that 'when the reformation of an abuse threatens to trench upon the convenience of the public, it is hard indeed to mend the matter'. He suggests that late hours of closing are new and that 'our grandfathers were wiser', and closed at 5 or 6pm. Fierce competition, consequent upon the existence of more shops than were needed, had brought the change. As banks in Liverpool closed at 1pm on Saturdays and as cotton brokers contemplated the same procedure, and as mechanics and artisans had a ten hour day, Flower felt that shop-assistants should receive consideration and that 'their labours should be limited to ten working hours a day, terminating not later than seven in the evening, and that the same rule should apply to every day in the week, and throughout the whole year'. Flower rejected a suggestion which had been made of an appeal to Parliament for legislation because he felt that it would be unsuccessful, unless supported by a large number of employers, and he doubted whether English ideas of freedom would allow legal regulation.[3]

Flower's zeal roused the Earl of Sefton and 1,700 citizens to persuade the Mayor of Liverpool to convene a public meeting on the subject of shop hours.[4] This took place on 10 April 1844 and passed a resolution, undoubtedly inspired by Flower, supporting a 7pm closing of shops.

The meeting empowered a committee of twelve ministers of religion and eight laymen, under the chairmanship of the mayor, to devise means of implementing the resolution. This committee held frequent meetings and sent 32,000 copies of appeals to the inhabitants and tradesmen. The assistants set up ten district committees, which sometimes met at 6am, to aid the work of propaganda. Yet no lasting change for the better seems to have followed.

Meanwhile, what of London? As long ago as 1825 a meeting of shopkeepers at the London Coffee House was held on 19 August to consider closing shops at an earlier hour. *The Times*, in a comment on the previous day, said, 'From seven in the morning until eleven at night our correspondent informs us that many of those individuals in the trade of linen-drapers are kept at work, without longer interval than one hour, all meals included, throughout the day'.[5] It must be remembered that these hours were for a six-day week—nobody thought about a half-holiday for workers in those days. *The Times* expressed surprise that young men were prepared to submit to such 'severe confinement' and it expressed even greater surprise that men were employed in shops at all, considering that shop work should be left to women.

The hundred or so linen-drapers, silk mercers, haberdashers and hosiers at the meeting passed a motion, with only three dissentients, suggesting that suitable closing hours for their shops would be 7pm for the first five nights of the week from 1 November to the end of February; 8pm in March, April, September and October; and 9pm in the remaining summer months. On Saturdays the time was to be one hour later in each group.[6]

On 23 August a meeting of shop-assistants approved this scale of hours and drew up a plan for a registry of the assistants and the establishment of a fund to support them in sickness or upon dismissal or retirement, or when 'any masters were found to contravene the regulations now adopted'.[7]

This was brave pioneering within so short a time of the repeal of the Combination Laws the previous year, a repeal due, in no small measure, to the work of a London tailor, Francis Place. Yet this seems to have been but a brief spark of zeal which soon flickered out. An attempt to re kindle the fire was the issue in 1839 by an anonymous writer of a publication called the *Linen Drapers' Magna Charta, or an Easy and Pleasant Mode of Diminishing Shopkeepers' Confinement*. It is said that, for £50 a year, a day of sixteen to eighteen hours was worked, a day rarely finishing before 9pm in winter and 11pm in summer. The remedy proposed was the formation of a metropolitan association of young men engaged in the retail drapery trade. Such an association, which could expect a membership of 15,000 and a yearly income of £15,000, should enforce a rule that no member worked for an employer whose other assistants were not all association members—an early suggestion of the closed shop! Its income would not only enable it to provide comfortable board and lodging for members thrown out of work but would support a hospital and institutions to promote music, drawing and physical exercise. Its aim, which would include the formation of provincial associations, would be to force Parliament to take notice of it and pass a law to compel drapers' shops to close at 7pm. Then the assistants in other trades, including the milliners, would imitate them.[8] This was far too bold a suggestion to be adopted by any shop-assistants in the climate of early Victorian England.

The writer of this book had, in part, been inspired by the formation in 1838 of the Metropolitan Drapers' Association which, he claimed, had achieved little. By 1842 this association had drawn up a set of rules which aimed at shortening the hours of work in the drapery and other trades in London, 'with a view to the physical, moral and intellectual improvement of the Assistants'.[9] The list of vice-patrons of the association was impressive—no patron had been secured—headed as it was by Lord Ashley, MP, and including Sir Andrew Agnew. There are interesting links here with the movement to secure better conditions in industry and a better observance of Sunday. There is no need to labour the work of Lord Ashley, better known to most people as the Earl of Shaftesbury, but the life-work of Sir Andrew Agnew is less well-known.[10]

Sir Andrew had worked in the House of Commons and outside to secure a better observance of Sunday in this country. Too often those who desired a Sunday in keeping with the English tradition of a day of rest and a day for worship were accused of opposition to enjoyment and recreation. Sir Andrew's name among the pioneers of shorter hours, together with that of Lord Ashley, who was also a great supporter of Sunday observance, shows that advocates of the claims of Sunday as a day apart were in the forefront of the movement for greater opportunities for recreation on the week-day. Indeed, the connection and the interplay between the movements for Sunday observance and shorter hours will be evident very frequently in the story of the efforts to secure shorter hours and a half-holiday for shopworkers.

The president of the Metropolitan Early Closing Association was Sir James Emerson Tennent and he was supported by some sixty vice-presidents among whom were Anglican clergy and Nonconformist ministers. One of the latter was the well-known Jabez Bunting, DD, and no doubt his influence led the Wesleyan Methodist Conference, meeting in Birmingham in July 1844, to pass a resolution of leisurely length which reflects the early Victorian ecclesiastical attitude to social problems. Under the heading 'Late Hours of Evening-Business in Shops etc' it reads:

> The Conference, having had their attention invited to this subject, cannot but feel that it involves, in various ways, high moral and religious considerations, and has a direct bearing on the intellectual improvement and spiritual prosperity of a large and interested class of society, especially of the respectable and well-principled young men employed in shops. They therefore commend the case to the calm and kindly regard of our members and friends whom it may concern; and will greatly rejoice if, by moderation, quiet perseverance, and united counsels, some means shall be devised for remedying, in whole or part, this obvious and serious evil—so as to secure the comfort and eventual advantage of all parties, and increase, in so far as may be practicable, the opportunities of a profitable attendance on the week-day ordinance of religion, and the appointed means of grace.[11]

To return to 1842 and the rules of the Metropolitan Early Closing Association, we find that the preface to the rules states that the majority of shops rarely closed before 11pm or midnight in summer and 10pm or 11pm in winter—the worst offenders being the drapers. The rules themselves were vague—no closing hours were suggested, only that 'an abridgement of the hours of business' be the aim. To achieve this, meetings and lectures were to be arranged, sermons to be preached, an appeal was to be made to the public, through the press, 'to abstain from shopping in the evening'. Representations were to be made to employers of the evils of late hours and the benefits of early closing. Finally, efforts were to be made to impress on the assistants the importance of using their free time to improve their mental faculties through literary institutes, attendance at lectures and the use of libraries. Thus was set out what were to be the guiding principles of the Early Closing Association, as it soon came to be known, for many years.

Thomas Davies, in an essay published in 1843, which won the prize offered by the Metropolitan Early Closing Association for 'the best practical Essay on the Evils of the present Protracted Hours of Trade generally, but more especially as they affect the Physical, Moral and Intellectual Condition of the Drapers of the Metropolis and the Advantage likely to arise from an Abridgement in reference to the Employed, the Employer, and the Public', gives a fairly complete picture of the hours and conditions then obtaining in London. He says that drapers' assistants work from 'six, seven, or eight o'clock in the morning, to nine, ten, eleven, or twelve o'clock in the evening; these variations being according to the season, the character of the shop, and the custom of the neighbourhood'. Shops were open longer in summer than winter, those that catered for the middle and working classes were open longer than those catering for the upper classes, those in busy streets kept longer hours than those in quieter streets.

In the best shops, the young men arrive to prepare the departments at 7am. They are followed at 7.30 or 8am by the seniors and then the younger men retire to dress in their serving attire, being allowed half an hour for this. A shop-assistant in such a place of business was, of course, expected to be faultlessly dressed even on a poor wage. The only breaks, after this, in the hours spent in the shop were five to ten minutes for breakfast and a similar time for tea, while dinner was snatched when it was possible to have it. The shop closes between 8 and 9pm in winter and an hour later in summer but after the shop is shut there is work to do in clearing up and this may take from one to three hours according to the nature and rush of business in the day. The assistants may not sit down, even if trade is slack, and they naturally suffer from the confined atmosphere, long hours of standing, and long hours of working in gas or oil lighting.

One hardly needs to be told by Davies that out of 700 members of the Mechanics' Institute in Southampton Buildings, only one is a linen-draper. Employers usually refused to employ married men and if this were not so the hours of business would prevent any real home life. Davies says that where possible the assistants stay in bed on Sunday morning and spend the rest of the time in getting such exercise as the season permits—skating, walking, boating, bathing, or reading.

Davies says that he has known 'houses of business in which, out of forty or fifty young men, not more than five or six have attended a place of worship during the Sunday'. No wonder the wiser clergy saw the need to support the claims for time for recreation in the week so that there might be the inclination to worship on Sunday. The various branches of the Christian church lost a great opportunity when they failed officially to use the weight of their authority to demand that employers and the public should alter their outlook on business.

It was estimated, by Davies, that probably a thousand young women, in the drapery trade in London, worked under similar conditions to the men.

By way of remedy for the conditions which he describes Davies suggests that masters who decide to close earlier than the normal time should display a notice in the window: 'This shop is closed at seven o'clock from motives of justice and humanity to the assistants.' He goes on to point out that many employers work nearly as long hours as their employees, that the cost of gas lighting is high, and that, while the heat injures some fabrics, the heat and light spoil the colours of others.[12]

The Hon and Rev Baptist W. Noel, MA, who was one of the judges for the competition in which Davies was successful, was a leading evangelical clergyman, and one of the queen's chaplains. He wrote a preface to the winning essay in which he pointed out that the age of the men in drapers' shops ranged from sixteen to thirty and that the conditions for druggists, grocers, milliners and dressmakers were similar to, or worse than, those described by Davies. Noel suggested that shops should open at 7am and close at 6pm to enable the assistants to be free by 7pm. He appealed to ministers of religion to exhort employers in their congregations to curtail the hours of work, but he felt that the final remedy was in the hands of the customers, to whom he appealed to shop by daylight only and at those shops which closed early.[13]

The efforts to secure shorter hours were not to achieve success by appeals to employers or shoppers on the grounds of humanity, justice or expediency, although it was to be a long time before those who campaigned for better conditions recognised this. There was one writer who, in 1843, realised something of the opposition to be met. The Rev J. Johns of Liverpool, who supported the efforts there of the shop-assistants, warned them that *'custom*, inveterate custom, is the great obstacle in your way'. This would hamper employers, employees and the public.

> The employers, in numberless cases, will object to your attempted reformation, that they have been accustomed to it all their lives, as their fathers were before them, and that they cannot think it wrong to keep up the good old practice. The employed, the assistants themselves, have been so long habituated to the yoke, that it has marked its palsying pressure upon their characters. The public immemorially used to exact attendance at all hours, will not readily admit the possibility of doing without the full liberty of the past.[14]

He shrewdly pointed out that the pioneers of change would be faced with the argument—to be repeated constantly in the following years—that the assistants would abuse any time of leisure. He does not believe they will but goes to the heart of the matter when he says that if the principle is right that the assistant, as a human being, is entitled to more leisure, then it is wrong not to give him that leisure, irrespective of the use made of it.

Yet between 1844 and 1850 things seemed to be on the move in the direction of shorter hours. Similar associations to the London Early Closing Association started in Manchester, Leeds, Bradford, Huddersfield, Coventry, Northampton, Birmingham,

Liverpool, Newcastle, Brighton, Portsmouth, Exeter and 'almost every town of importance in the kingdom'.[15]

The Metropolitan Association itself was a promoter of much local activity, sponsoring meetings and issuing appeals. As early as September 1843 the linen drapers of the City agreed to close at 8pm in that month and in October and at 7pm in the following four months. Outside the City the firms of Swan and Edgar in Piccadilly, Redmayne of Bond Street, Peters and Underwood of Sloane Square promised to do the same.[16] A meeting held in February 1844 carried with acclamation a resolution to secure the same hours in Bishopsgate and Shoreditch.[17]

In November 1845, Mr T. Wakley, MP, at a meeting of the association in the famous Exeter Hall, could say, 'the middle class having begun to extend their support, and having the countenance of religion, failure was impossible'. He added, 'If avarice should rear its hideous head against the best principles of humanity, the Legislature must put a stop to it.'[18] Probably as a legislator the phrase came easily to his lips, although as an ardent worker for reform both inside and outside Parliament he can hardly have been optimistic about quick results. He was a medical practitioner in London, who founded the *Lancet*, and he had made a great impression in the House of Commons by a speech supporting the Tolpuddle Martyrs. Thus the association, by securing him as a speaker, had, as often, obtained the support of a well-known sympathiser with those suffering injustice.

By the following month the association was arranging a series of district meetings to promote the cause of early closing. At the first, held in a room in Commercial Road, Stepney, the chairman estimated that 50,000 young men and women, between the ages of fifteen and twenty-five years, were employed in shops in the metropolis—drapers, grocers, chemists, etc—and that there were 77,000 shopkeepers.[19] An appeal to discontinue late shopping moved the ladies to stand as an expression of their determination to support the cause. One wonders if many of them were accustomed to shop late in any case, although their maids might do so and might continue so to do without, or even with, the knowledge of their mistresses.

On 18 December, Mr Wakley presided at a public soirée arranged by the association at Hanover Square. He said that it was the largest tea party which he had attended, some 500 ladies and gentlemen being present.[20] The movement for early closing was well launched socially.

At the beginning of 1846 the association launched an appeal for £5,000 to pursue the object of earlier closing.[21] A well-known figure amongst the Wesleyan Methodists, the Rev William Arthur, was one of the chief speakers at the meeting at Crosby Hall, in Bishopsgate Street, at which the appeal was made and he claimed that it was admitted that a number of deaths among young shop-employees could be attributed to the long hours of work. He refuted as fictitious the belief that longer hours of leisure would corrupt the morals of the young men. The idea that long hours of work were really beneficial, because they kept people out of temptation, was a convenient prop to the Victorian doctrine of the virtue of hard work.

In the January issue of the *Evangelical Magazine*, in 1845, an article on 'The Curtailment of Business Hours' paid tribute to the work of the Metropolitan Association and echoed the prevailing optimism that its success was assured. The association, 'by prudent and wise measures', has enlightened the public mind, allayed apprehension on the score of economy and proved that its plan of operation is 'peaceful, humane, and strictly voluntary'. Let it so continue and every shop will be shut at a reasonable hour and it will secure for the young assistants 'sufficient leisure for self-improvement, and annihilate the species of refined slavery which has too long obtained in various departments of mercantile life'.[22]

In March 1847 the Exeter Hall was full for the fifth annual meeting of the Metropolitan Early Closing Association when the Marquis of Westminster presided, supported by several members of Parliament. One speaker gave an interesting glimpse of one of the minor hindrances to success when he said that, as an employer, he had tried to get his fellow employers to agree to close at 7pm, and all but one were prepared to do this. The exception said, 'What can I do from seven o'clock till eleven? I can't read.'

Several speakers referred to the passing by the House of Commons on that day of the bill fixing a ten-hour day for young people in factories but not one of them drew the conclusion that if legislation had been necessary for factory reform it would also be required to secure shop reform. One speaker stated quite clearly that the association was not asking for parliamentary action. Examples of long hours were quoted—the fishmongers worked from 4am to 9pm with additional Sunday work; bakers often had an eighteen- or twenty-hour day. A fresh suggestion came from a speaker who advocated the payment of wages on Friday instead of Saturday because shops in artisan areas had to keep open late on Saturday if wages were not paid until Saturday afternoon or evening.[23]

When the next annual meeting came, under the chairmanship of the lord mayor, a note was struck which was to echo down the century—the apathy of the young men assistants to the work of the association. In contrast to the previous year there was the suggestion of Mr C. Hindley, MP, that the association should work for an act of Parliament fixing a twelve-hour day, meal times included, with terms of pay fixed for these hours and overtime pay for any additional hours. Not surprisingly this met with no support.[24]

The association planned meetings to rouse the interest of the assistants. One was held for those working in Chelsea, Pimlico and adjacent areas in January 1848. The object was to obtain support for the closing of all shops at 7pm each evening. The secretary of the Early Closing Association, John Lilwall, suggested that every householder should receive a copy of the prize essay on the evils of late hours of business and that then they could be canvassed to sign a pledge promising that neither they nor their servants would shop after 7pm. A large meeting of assistants carried a resolution to implement such a scheme, proposed by a surgeon, who pointed out the physical dangers of working fourteen and sixteen hours a day behind a counter.[25] One is left wondering to what extent the resolution was made effective. How many assistants had the energy to canvass, and how were they received at a late hour in the evening? At any rate there is no evidence that any success was more than very short-lived.

Meanwhile hours were being reduced in the warehouses, offices and the wholesale trade. In 1844 warehousemen in the City of London were combining to secure shorter hours and a mid-day closing on Saturdays, and forty leading wholesalers agreed to close at 6pm each evening.[26] But in the wholesale grocery, tea, coffee and spice trade this struggle for a 6pm closing was still going on in 1848.[27] City of London and West End banks closed at 4pm daily by the end of that year.[28] In Manchester the banks, solicitors' offices, local government offices and warehouses had secured a 4pm daily closing by the end of 1848.[29] In Bristol, Samuel Budgett was the pioneer of earlier hours in the wholesale grocery trade and before his death, in 1851, his warehouse closed by 5.30pm and sometimes 5pm. He knew his London as well as Bristol and considered that, whereas there had been a shortening of hours in the high-class shops, 'the most protracted hours are still persisted in by the greater part of the grocers, chemists, oilmen, tobacconists' and shops of every type in the poorer areas.[30]

It was in keeping with the general outlook of the mid-century years that the Early Closing Association should feel that there was to be inevitable progress to complete success and, in keeping with the general picture of the fifties, little or no permanent progress was made. The 1850s saw a lull in social reform.[31] The Great Exhibition of 1851 demonstrated to native and foreigner alike the greatness of Britain's manufacturing power. Out of the wealth that it epitomised must assuredly stem, at the appropriate time, benefits for all who had contributed to it by their dutiful labour. Such was the philosophy of the hour.

CHAPTER THREE

JOHN LILWALL AND THE HALF-HOLIDAY

The Early Closing Association, from almost its start until the end of the 1850s, was to a great extent directed and encouraged by its very energetic honorary secretary, John Lilwall. Not only did he seize every opportunity to campaign in the Metropolitan area but he was instrumental in starting, or inspiring the right people to start, similar associations in other parts of the country.

In April 1855 Lilwall was in touch with a law stationer, J. R. Taylor, who wanted the association to take up the matter of a half-holiday for shopworkers. The efforts of Taylor and Lilwall led to a public meeting in the Guild Hall on 15 August, when nearly 4,000 people turned up, only half of that number being able to gain admittance. The subject had been mooted before, and tried in various places and among other groups of workers as we have seen, but Taylor claimed that this was the first time that the subject of a half-holiday for London shops was put prominently before the public. A resolution was carried by acclamation,

That early closing on Saturdays having been already adopted in

D

Edinburgh, Glasgow, and the principal towns in Scotland, also in Liverpool, Manchester, Leeds and other places in the north of England, as well as by some important branches of business in London, and the result having proved to be highly beneficial to large classes of society, socially, mentally, and physically; added to the most important effect of tending materially to a better observance of the Lord's day; these facts afford safe grounds for assuming that such measures must prove a national benefit, and that this Meeting has, therefore, the greatest confidence in recommending it for general adoption.

It was suggested that shops should close at 2pm on Saturdays.

By February 1857 Taylor had secured his immediate object for the workers in solicitors' and other law offices, for after much correspondence the lord chancellor made an order making proceedings after 2pm on a Saturday null and void and no writs were to be issued after that hour. The Early Closing Association tried to get the Home Secretary, Sir George Grey, to commit the government to use its influence to see that government offices, dockyards etc closed at 2pm but it was told that it was not practicable.[1] As far as ordinary shops were concerned the chief result was that the association was now committed to campaigning for a half-holiday.

The way minds were speculating on the half-holiday is illustrated by some lectures given in the winter of 1855-6, in a series arranged by the YMCA. The lecturer, James Miller, professor of surgery in the University of Edinburgh, argued that man's day was meant to be divided into three eight-hour portions, one for work, one for sleep, and one for recreation, with Sunday as a rest day. He felt this was too revolutionary a doctrine for his generation to accept and so he suggested, as a compromise, a day of ten hours' work, eight hours' sleep and six hours' recreation. He suggested that every employer should take a holiday of thirty-one continuous days in the year. His imagination did not carry him as far as a conception of a fortnight or three weeks' holiday with pay for employees so he proposed that employees should have a half-holiday every week, which would equal twenty-six days'

holiday in a year, together with another five days completely free
from work. He said: 'Early closing is the key to the family altar,
and the Saturday half-holiday is the key to the Sabbath. The
Saturday afternoon is the time for recreation; that is the time for
steamboat trips and cheap railway trains, and for opening Crystal
Palaces and British Museums. That is the time for throwing
open, too, the public gardens, with their military bands.'[2]

Miller opposed a device suggested by some people of 'buying
a half-holiday on Saturday by working longer periods on other
days'. The prevailing climate of laissez-faire prevented Miller
seeing that the employers, of themselves, would never attain his
ideal. He no doubt amused his audience, but he did not offer a
practical solution to an ever-recurring obstacle to better conditions when he said that in a case where a single shopkeeper in a
town had prevented the other apothecaries putting into operation
a half-holiday, those who wanted the plan 'should have rolled
him in a globular form, like one of his own pills, and swallowed
him at once. I don't believe he would ever have been felt.'

The YMCA, started in 1844, under whose auspices Miller had
lectured, had of necessity close connection with the Early Closing
Association. The YMCA could provide for the leisure hours of
male employees but its cultural facilities would be unused if no
leisure was secured.

About 1855 a spirited attack on the Early Closing Association
was published by one who called himself 'A Ten Years'
Subscriber' to the body. It is a single sheet of comments on
an address which had been issued by the association to the
assistants. The author refuted the excuse that late hours of
opening resulted from people wanting or needing to shop late
by claiming that by staying open late shops attracted late shoppers. He demanded that competition between rivals for late
business should end—banks and offices did not vie with each
other in this way. He wanted much more publicity and an effort
to secure legislation. He touched on another evil of much of the
shop organisation of that time when he attacked employers for

refusing to engage married men or women, for thus 'they compel thousands of the Assistants, of both sexes, to live in a disgusting, immoral, and most unnatural state of celibacy, and then complain of the want of morals'.[3] Apparently his attack had no influence on the association—one of its weaknesses was that it had little real support from, or understanding of, the assistants. It was too complacent and too patronising in its attitude to them.

John FitzGerald published a book in 1856 which, while pleading for shorter hours and a Saturday half-holiday for everyone, made special mention of the workers in retail shops. This work was greatly influenced by all that John Lilwall was advocating but it brought a fresh outlook, and a very modern one, to the subject. A cricket ground in every village was the writer's desire and he hoped 'that our landowners will soon begin to set apart play fields for their poor neighbours'.[4] He admits that the Early Closing Association had had some success in London but pointed to the opposition of the individual who stood out of a voluntary agreement, and so wrecked it, and referred to the large number of small tradesmen who kept their shops open very late and who opened for half the day on Sunday. He mentioned that in Manchester most of the merchants and wholesale shopkeepers closed at 2pm on Saturday. Solicitors' offices in Manchester, Cambridge and some other places closed at 1pm on Saturday[5] and in York at 1pm on Wednesday.[6]

FitzGerald concludes: 'Let those of us who are living in affluence resolve to buy what articles we want during the first five and a half days of the week. Let us not buy anything after six in the evening. Let us enter no shop on a Saturday afternoon. Let us pay the wages of all our workmen on Friday evening at latest.'[7] But what of the great majority of customers who were not affluent and whose needs kept open the small shops? So, too, FitzGerald failed to estimate the magnitude of the problem and he did not realise that the social conscience of the people generally had not been sufficiently trained in self-discipline to enable voluntary methods to succeed.

It is now time to look at John Lilwall's own book, based upon material which he had collected, illustrating the shop hours prevailing in many parts of the country. The book, *The Half-Holiday Question*, was only sixty-two pages long in its revised second edition, published in 1856, but it showed clearly how the shopworkers lagged behind the majority of the employees in commerce, the professions and industry and also how timid was the faith of those who were working to improve conditions for them. Thus Lilwall says that in the opinion of his committee a 7pm winter closing and an 8pm summer closing was the best that could be hoped for 'at least for some years to come', for retail shops, while admitting that wholesale firms closed earlier on five days and at 2pm on Saturday.[8]

Lilwall concluded that a uniform 2pm closing on one day a week was not possible and he revealed another weakness of his association, namely its dominance by the interests of the large business house and its inability to appreciate the circumstances of the owner with only one or two assistants, when he suggested that some assistants might be given a half-holiday one week and some another, subject, also, to whether trade was brisk or slack.[9]

The idea, later to materialise as the Bank Holiday, that four, or five, whole-day holidays a year would be beneficial is put forward by Lilwall but he does not favour the suggestion that there should be a dozen or more such holidays of a single day at a time. He felt that such a scheme would prevent any hope of a weekly half-holiday, and so 'may be likened to the almost overfeeding of men on rare or isolated occasions, allowing them, during the other part of the year, barely enough food to sustain life'.[10]

One of the unfortunate attitudes of the mid-Victorian era is admitted by Lilwall as early as 1856 when he writes: 'We have, as a people, allowed ourselves to be engrossed by the occupation of money-getting, to the neglect of pursuits of a more refined and elevated character.'[11] That is why he devotes some space in his book to showing that those workers who have shorter hours and a half-holiday use their leisure time in healthy outdoor recreation or in the facilities provided by the YMCA, the Metropolitan Evening Classes and Mutual Improvement Societies. Lilwall is at pains to stress, also, that not until there are shorter hours, and particularly a half-holiday, can shopworkers be expected to spend their Sundays in the way so many Christian people desired. 'Debar them during the week from seeing the blue sky and inhaling Heaven's sweet breezes, and vain will be the attempt to secure their uniform, if even occasional, attendance at the House of Prayer—so long, in fact, will it be hopeless to expect that they will refrain from taking their amusement on the Lord's Day, and devote its sacred hours to those calmer and holier enjoyments and pursuits for which it was in mercy consecrated and set aside.'[12]

By the mid-1850s the necessity of factory legislation was accepted and no one had fought harder to secure a limitation of hours for women and children, and so, indirectly, for men, than the Earl of Shaftesbury. Yet he was not prepared to seek the help of the law for the shopworker. He was in the chair at a meeting, in the organisation of which Lilwall's work can be seen, which was held in London on 24 April 1856 to consider the matter of a Saturday half-holiday and the earlier payment of wages. Lord Shaftesbury said: 'We do not contemplate legislation. Legislation here would be altogether inapplicable.'[13] The official resolution carried at the meeting advocated the payment of wages on Friday evening or early on Saturday, but in moving it the Rev William Arthur, the well-known Wesleyan Methodist leader, gave as his own view the suggestion that Monday morning would be a more suitable time. His reasons for this were that the housewife would have the money to spend when the week's needs began to require it being spent and that the men would attend work on Monday —as sometimes they did not—in order to draw their wages.

This natural concern of the shopkeeper about the time when wages were paid reminds us that many factors, outside the control of the shopowner, had a bearing on any reform of shop hours.

It was the Rev William Arthur, too, who suggested that the level of the tone of outdoor and indoor recreations would be raised when those of a religious bent, now not prepared to take part on Sunday, were free to participate on Saturday afternoon.

Lilwall was able to give an impressive report of the activities of the Early Closing Association at its annual meeting which packed the Exeter Hall in London in September 1856. The chairman on that occasion was Samuel Morley, the Congregational millionaire and philanthropist, who rather naïvely regretted that the profit motive was so mixed with the subject of shop hours. He claimed that: 'The question was rather a moral one. They had to consider that they were dealing with those who had minds as well as bodies. The fact was that at the present time they were all living too fast, doing as much now in one hour as they used formerly to do in two.'[14] In spite of the enthusiasm and moral fervour it was admitted that not much improvement could be recorded in the hours of retail shops.

Under Lilwall's guidance the Early Closing Association announced in 1853 that it was setting up a home in London for young shopwomen seeking employment. This would meet a real need, for when the majority of women 'lived in' an employee put up with bad conditions rather than give up a job which would mean that she had nowhere to live and insufficient money to obtain lodgings while seeking fresh employment. At the meeting, held in March, at which this project was announced the lord mayor, who presided, had used the words 'white slavery' in reference to the long hours prevailing in the shops.[15] This expression probably led a woman who signed herself 'A First Hand' to write a long letter to *The Times* exposing the conditions in the first-class millinery and dressmaking houses. She had been in such houses for fourteen years and her health was now suffering from the effects of long hours of work. In one West End house she had had twelve young girls under her. For some weeks, in late May and early June each year, the hours for work and meals were as follows. Breakfast, for which only fifteen minutes was allowed, was at 6am. Then work began. At 11am a small piece of dry bread was brought round to each person for lunch. Dinner was at 1 o'clock and twenty minutes only was allowed for it. Only twice a week was hot meat included in this meal, there was no pudding, and there was toast and a glass of water to drink. At 5pm fifteen minutes was allowed for tea and at 9pm another fifteen minutes for a supper of bread, dry cheese and a glass of beer. Work continued after that until 1am, 2am or sometimes 3am except on Saturday when work stopped at midnight. As a result of this period of work the writer was ill for three months. Her wages as a first hand were £40 a year. A second-hand dressmaker was paid £14 a year and a second-hand milliner £24. A saleswoman received £20. All the others paid a premium to learn the business.[16]

In a later letter the same writer referred to the fact that often six, eight or ten girls or young women slept in one room with not even a chimney for ventilation. In the same issue of the paper a letter signed 'Newington' claimed that similar conditions existed in many houses of business.[17]

A third letter from 'First Hand' said that, because of the long hours at all seasons, few young people employed in business attended a place of worship on Sunday. In the morning they slept and then visited friends for the rest of the day, but she also hinted that some, without friends at hand, fell to what she called the allure of the seducer. She had remonstrated with some of these girls only to receive the reply, 'Oh, anything to get out of these dens of toil'.[18]

In 1855 a select committee of the House of Lords, presided over by the Earl of Shaftesbury, published evidence on conditions in the millinery and dressmaking trade. One of the witnesses, R. D. Grainger, had been a royal commissioner in 1842 inquiring into the same subject. He was a lecturer in physiology at St Thomas's Hospital and he said that there had been little improvement between 1842 and 1855. He said that on the good side could be put the ending of Sunday work and the fact that it was unusual for young persons to work all night. Yet young people, he testified, worked fifteen or more hours a day.

These workers were not, of course, shop-assistants but their work was so closely linked with that of the assistants that it merits attention. Those who defended the long hours did so on the grounds of the whims of fashion or of the Court: ladies cannot order Court dresses long in advance as the fashion is not then known. The queen often gives but short notice of a move to Windsor and ladies of the Court need special dresses quickly. The work is so seasonal that one witness, a dressmaker, gave holidays of several weeks' duration to her staff when there was no work. Another witness, with a wide knowledge of the trade, said that foreign business houses in London were better conducted than English ones. Yet another witness said that employees, aged thirteen to twenty-five, worked from 8am to 2am in the season. Many of these were apprentices for whom a premium of £40 to £60 had been paid. One witness said that she had worked, in the season, from 6am to midnight with only ten minutes for breakfast at 7am, and the same time at 2pm for dinner. With reference to her fellow workers she said: 'I have seen them sit and faint and left to come to as they liked, or as they could, and no notice was taken of them.'[19]

In spite of disappointments and set-backs, Lilwall and the Early Closing Association decided, in 1857, that a sufficient number of the larger London business houses were giving a Saturday afternoon holiday to their young men to warrant an approach to the directors of the Crystal Palace Company to arrange special Saturday afternoon fêtes. The first was held on 15 August. Rain spoilt a cricket match between eleven clerks and eleven warehousemen—probably both classes outnumbered the shop-assistants who were free—but the bands of the Scots Fusilier Guards and the Crystal Palace Company played inside, there was a concert, and an organ recital. Cricket enthusiasts and correspondents may note that *The Times,* referring to the match, said, 'We need not enter into the minutae of this sport, for cricket is but a dull game to the lookers on, and its interest is by no means heightened in the narration'.[20]

By 1858 the chief successes of the association had been in warehouses and offices, not in shops. For example, the offices of the British and Foreign Bible Society, the works of the Eastern Counties Railway Company, the Gutta Percha Company in City Road, Chubb and Sons the lock-manufacturers (in Wolverhampton and London), and certain wholesale druggists and clothiers in the City of London were closing by 2pm on Saturday. So, too, were the wholesale booksellers in Paternoster Row by 1859. Attempts to get the London banks to close were still being made in 1859 but had succeeded in Manchester, Liverpool and Bristol.[21]

It is not always possible to trace a direct connection between the work of Lilwall and attempts to obtain shorter hours in various parts of the country. Where there was not an actual link with London the climate of opinion there was bound to affect other places. For example in York, in 1854, the grocers' assistants petitioned their employers to close at 7pm instead of 8pm each evening. A local paper said that many grocers were favourable, so 'we trust their assistants will soon possess this small addition to their time for recreation and mental improvement'. What followed is not recorded but in the following month, October, an advertisement in the *Yorkshireman* indicated that hatters, tailors and outfitters in York would close at 7pm each evening from 16 October to 10 March 1855.[22] Again no further references can be traced so we cannot tell whether this was the light that soon flickered out or one that continued in a regular glow.

In Leicester there was an Early Closing Association, which almost certainly means that Lilwall's influence had been operative to some extent. It was strong enough to offer prizes for essays on the subject of early closing and to publish winning ones. One of these, published in 1855, reflects the optimism of the age for, after referring to the evils of late hours, William Smeeton writes: 'Fortunately it is not likely that this evil will be perpetuated, for already the attention of the nation is turned to the subject; early closing associations are forming in most of our large towns, and there seems to be a growing conviction in society both of the rectitude and policy of their endeavours.' He adds a word of warning to the Christian employers (and few employers would have repudiated the adjective), which was for the most part to go unheeded. He suggests that forcing young employees to work long hours is not in accord with the commandment, 'Love thy neighbour as thyself', and poses the query, 'Will not young men ask for some stronger proof of the Christianity of their employers?' [23]

The strength of the parent Early Closing Association, as of others that had a transitory success, was in the wealth and influence of the employers who supported it. Its weakness was in the lack of solid support by the employees, and by the small shop-keepers. For example, in 1852 the London association was in debt and hampered by lack of funds until Mr Hitchcock, a silk mercer of St Paul's Churchyard, promised to double the sum members raised. They raised £406, Mr Hitchcock gave £406, the debt was cleared and there was over £500 for new work.[24] Mr Hitchcock was one of those enlightened employers who, as he said in 1853 at a meeting of the association, 'had closed early, provided better apartments, given longer holidays, and otherwise increased the comforts of his young men for the last ten years, and he found that doing so, paid'.[25] The example of such men might be admired but few imitated—as few factory-owners had dared to imitate Robert Owen.

A near neighbour of Mr Hitchcock in St Paul's Churchyard, Mr James Spence, in 1859 offered a prize through the association of fifty guineas for the best essay on the subject of a Saturday half-holiday and the early payment of wages. Fifty-six essays were submitted and the winning one, by John Dennis, was published in 1860. He devoted one chapter to the importance of Sunday and the way in which the neglect of worship and the use of Sunday for pleasure was a necessary consequence of late hours on Saturday. He regarded the half-holiday—meaning early-closing on Saturday—as a means of arresting Sunday desecration. He claimed that nearly half the shops in London were open after 10am on Sunday and that in some neighbourhoods almost every shop was open.[26]

Increasing emphasis was put, by those anxious to see a better observance of Sunday, on the need for early closing on Saturday. A layman and a clergyman stressed this point at a public meeting in St James's Hall held by the Early Closing Association in the summer of 1860. At this meeting it was suggested that if shops closed early young men shop-assistants would join the Rifle Volunteer movement. Thus was patriotic fervour enlisted in the half-holiday movement while the chairman at the meeting, Lord Elcho, MP, himself a promoter of the Volunteer movement, made a special appeal to the ladies to refrain from Saturday afternoon shopping and join the seventy-three who had already signed a promise not to shop that afternoon.[27]

It was fear of the ambitions of Napoleon III which, in 1859, had prompted the formation of the Volunteer Corps. *Punch*, during 1860, contained cartoons highlighting the humorous side of the zeal to volunteer and in one of its August numbers had an article under the heading 'Soldiering and Shopping'. It drew the attention of the ladies to a paragraph in one of the morning papers relating that a number of West End tradesmen were considering closing early at 4pm in winter and 5pm in summer every Saturday. The paper supported a 2pm closure every Saturday but significantly commented that the suggestion was an innovation in the retail trade and so no doubt caution was wise. *Punch*, having given this information for the benefit of the ladies who would be more familiar with the pages of *Punch* than with a journal 'devoted more to politics and commerce', asked its readers to support the suggestion, chiefly in order to provide recruits for the Volunteers. The writer warms to his theme with the sentences:

> Let every mother of a family who has a wish to see her family defended from invasion, not only rigidly abstain from shopping

late herself, but take care to teach her daughters, as they grow, to do as she does. 'Shop early' should be one of the first texts in a girl's copybook, and no pains should be spared in impregnating her mind with it. Every 'bargain' which is bought after two o'clock on Saturday deprives a Rifleman, or would-be one, of practice at his drill, and diminishes thereby the defences of the country. [And almost as an afterthought] On the score, too, of humanity, late shopping should be stopped, and the Cruelty Prevention Society should see to it.[28]

Punch had been one of the early supporters of the shop-assistants in their struggle for shorter hours, for as early as 1843 the journal had advocated their cause.[29] In 1861 it returned to the subject of the connection with the Volunteers and decided that satirical invention might renew the interest of its readers in the needs of the shopworkers. Under the heading 'The Lady and the Volunteers', it produced a letter, purporting to come from Islington, from a lady who signed herself Honoria Dawdleton, happy to hear that a large city shopkeeper had forbidden his assistants to become Volunteers. The composition is worthy of reproduction in part because it shows *Punch*'s careful observation of the attitude of some of the ladies towards shop-assistants.

> Since the young men in the shops have taken to Volunteering, I have observed a marked change in their manners, and that change for the worse. They serve you, certainly, and I do not know that I can recollect any downright want of respect to me (I should soon have walked out of any shop if I had seen that) but I have noticed that when they have produced everything that I have asked for, and mentioned the price, and all about it, they seem to think that no more is required from them. One may take it, or leave it. There is much less eagerness to please, much less attempt to guide your judgement and persuade you that it is the very thing you want, much less of what—I call it *proper attention*, but what my husband (who is prejudiced) calls fawning and servility, but which, if one is a lady and has money in one's pocket, one has a right to expect from the lower orders. Shopping is not shopping, it is merely asking for what you want, buying it, and going away, and we like to be canvassed for our favours, as you do for your votes . . . One of these days we shall have the young men declin-

ing to sell ribbons and flannels, and declaring that it is work for girls. I should like to see myself in a shop with pert minxes waiting on me. Please support this shopkeeper, Mr Punch, and believe me,
                    Yours sincerely, Honoria Dawdleton.

PS. I suppose the Early Closing and the Volunteer business go together. I *choose* to shop in the evening when it is cool and pleasant, and when I have my husband (and his pence) with me. Besides, how can you buy colours, for evening wear, by daylight? It is preposterous. And how are poor servant-girls to manage? Ask any servant-girl if her sentiments are not the same as mine. And yet you call *yourself a friend* of the people![30]

Evidently the idea, expressed by *The Times* in 1825, that shop-assistants should be women, had gained little favour. Not that women shop-assistants were unknown but in the West End shops men predominated.

Clearly more than appeals to patriotism or humanity would be needed before the Early Closing Association could achieve its objectives. John Lilwall had given so much of his time and energy to the work of the association as its honorary secretary that in 1858 he had to consider resigning from this position in order to devote more time to his own affairs. This led to a subscription list being opened on his behalf and, of those who contributed, over eighty sent glowing tributes to Lilwall's skill and enthusiasm. These were published and included letters from the Earl of Shaftesbury, the bishops of Chichester and Oxford, the Rev William Arthur, secretary of the Wesleyan Methodist Missionary Society, and the Rev J. T. Baylee, the secretary of the Lord's Day Observance Society. Mr F. Larkins, in business in St Paul's Churchyard, wrote: 'When I first heard of Mr Lilwall in 1844 I was engaged regularly from 7am to 10.30pm all the year through. I have lived to see these long hours curtailed on an average from two to three hours per day.' Many declared that it was only the zeal of Lilwall which had kept the association in being.[31]

There can be no doubt that, although so much of what appeared to have been achieved was ephemeral, Lilwall's name deserves to be remembered among the pioneers of social reform in the mid-nineteenth century.

CHAPTER FOUR

THE DRAPER AND CLOTHIER
AND THE AGE OF COMPLACENCY

In May 1859 the first number of a monthly magazine, the *Draper and Clothier*, appeared. It aimed at being an 'organ of intercommunication and permanent record' for the drapers, mercers, haberdashers, hosiers, milliners, clothiers, tailors and other similar trades. It ceased publication with the April issue for 1862. Within that period, particularly from correspondence it published, the magazine tells us quite a lot about the attitude of the employers, especially to the Early Closing Association.

In the third number, in July 1859, an article was entitled, 'A Half-Holiday and late opening versus Early Closing'. The writer says that he felt at first that the Early Closing Association was 'the right association for the right place', but now he likens himself to Balaam, 'who would willingly bless, but is prohibited from so doing by a higher obligation'. He terms the association 'one of the many empirical suggestions of the day'. It is 'one of the pretty ideas of little minds, that are born to struggle and flounder from year to year, simply because it has been started on crude, unsound, illogical, and mischievous views and principles'. The writer justifies this statement on the grounds that to close shops at twilight and release half a million 'handsome young men' in London, Manchester, Liverpool and other large towns would be destructive of their best interests and those of their employers and society in general. Yet he cannot defend the existing long hours which he proposes should be shortened by shops opening at 9am instead of 8am with a weekly half-holiday. Such a proposal for later opening would not injure the employers for there is no early morning business. The employees would benefit, for 'the morning air is the purest; one long breath of it on Lord's cricket ground, on the Islington rifle ground, in Hyde Park, on Clapham Common, or on Hounslow Heath, at 7am, would be worth to them all that they could inhale, or otherwise obtain, from 7 to 12pm in all the crowded streets, smoking-rooms, theatres, gin palaces, and other similar places of resort in the world'. With a weekly half-holiday employees would be able to visit friends and have longer time for recreation and the pursuit of health and knowledge.[1]

The same number of the magazine has a letter signed 'A Shopkeeper' which is very critical of the Early Closing Association. He says that he is writing at the request of many small shopkeepers who are constantly charged by the large shopkeepers with holding up the move for shorter hours. Those he represents would close at 7pm in winter and 8pm in summer if the shops catering for the wealthy classes 'will close at five and six, so as to give us, the inferior shopkeepers, who keep but few hands, a small chance of picking up a few crumbs from customers who cannot get at the great drapers' counters in time'. Without such an arrangement the evil will continue. 'The Earl of Shaftesbury, prize essays, fêtes at the Crystal Palace, and elderly ladies, may brings funds to keep alive the ECA, but what we require is for the association to come to an end, and the evil also.'[2]

This letter illustrates the fact that the main support for the association came from the wealthier shopkeepers and it is significant that a letter which follows the one just quoted, support-

E

ing the association, is signed 'A Early Closer, Oxford Street'.

The September issue carried a second article, similar in tone and argument to the July one. There was also a long letter supporting the association from 'A Country Draper', saying that the employers who have tried the association's ideas have received more willing service from their employees. He praises the association because 'it has said, with an emphasis greatly needed, that man is something more than a working animal'. The letter points out that it would be impossible to get uniformity of hours—what suits one district would not suit another—and it condemns one of the methods used by the association, that of groups of ladies planning to influence and neutralise the hours of opening. If this means anything, 'it means intimidation as unmanly as it is unpolite'.[3]

A letter signed 'A Commercial', written in September 1859, expressed pleasure in seeing what the writer termed 'Titmice' assistants 'showing spirit'. He described how recently, 'at a fashionable wateringplace in Yorkshire', a shop-owner instructed his assistants at 8pm to re-dress the shop and windows in order to attract visitors who would pass the shop at 9pm on leaving a concert. The assistants refused or 'struck', and so 'the proprietor now sees the necessity of closing at the same hour as the rest of the trade in the town'.[4]

The same issue carried a spirited letter from an Oxford Street, London, assistant which voiced the frustration many assistants and employers must have felt. It read:

> Are we to have early closing, or not? or is it to be a half-holiday, and when? We want no more talk, no more writing; we wish acting, and at once. For twenty years we have been befooled out of our money to forward the cause; and now I am told by many if I will but belong to the 'Young Men's Christian Association' I shall assist very much in forwarding the early closing movement ... The law says how many hours the factory hands shall work— why not have the same law for drapery hands?[5]

But one example of the futility of achieving any permanent

solution of the problem by voluntary agreement comes from Woolwich. What happened there would not have been 'news' because it was so common, but for the uncommon sequel. A draper named Stone, in Powis Street, had agreed when approached by two assistants to close at 8pm in winter, if all the other drapers did the same. He did close at 8pm for a short time and then found that seven or eight other drapers remained open until nearly 8.30pm and so he remained open until 9pm. What was unusual was that some of the assistants then organised a crowd of some 200 to demonstrate outside Stone's shop between 8 and 9pm in the course of which his premises were damaged to the extent of £10 value. Four men were arrested and charged— they included Roger Langstaff, the secretary of the Woolwich Early Closing Association. Two were discharged on bail and two apologised and offered to pay for the damage.[6]

Correspondence on the merits or otherwise of early closing continued in the journal until July 1861 and then the subject was dropped. The general impression one gets is that the Early Closing Association was not achieving much at this time, that it was considered to be the instrument of the large shop-owners, whose opportunity for trade had really ceased by early evening, and that it took insufficient notice of the needs of the small shop-keepers, whose customers expected shopping facilities in the late evening.

One of the correspondents to the *Draper and Clothier* wished to abolish the Early Closing Association and substitute for it a 'Late Opening and Early Rising Association', thus developing a point made in the third number by an earlier writer. He maintained that employers would not mind opening an hour or two later if their assistants rose early to play cricket on Clapham Common or carry a rifle in Hyde Park. He himself, thirty or forty years ago, had risen at 5am to play cricket.[7] The reference to soldiering in Hyde Park was topical. As we have seen, the fear of a French invasion had led to a sudden zeal to form bodies of Volunteers to augment the regular forces. The desire to demonstrate their patriotism and harness its popular appeal to their cause no doubt led the officials of the Early Closing Association to invite the Inspector-General of Volunteers to preside at the annual meeting of the association in 1864.

Colonel McMurdo, CB, saw his opportunity to further his work, and he stated in his speech that he looked to the success of the movement, to close early and secure a half-holiday, to supply recruits for the Volunteers. Already, according to the colonel, one of the most efficient companies in one of the most efficient London regiments came from the employees of J. Shoolbred and Company.[8]

This new interest led *The Times* to report the meeting at length—having ignored the work of the association for some years—including a reference to a choir of 200 members of the association. The next annual meeting had a choir of 300 and Lord Lyttleton in the chair. He claimed that the upper classes often had more leisure than was good for them; the working classes, in general, did not require more leisure; but the middle classes, 'the class to which the great body of the members of the association belonged', were in great need of leisure.[9] Although the association was obviously established socially among the vast number of 'good causes' that attracted so much outward favour in mid-Victorian days its practical achievements seem rather hollow, as reported at that meeting. It was helping local committees in more than thirty towns and in London it could claim that a number of retail houses (not small shops) closed at 8pm in summer and 7pm in winter, while the Saturday half-holiday had made 'very satisfactory progress' in wholesale houses, and retail shops were closing at 4pm on Saturday in winter and 5pm in summer. This does not indicate much progress for years of effort; clearly the association was too complacent and easily satisfied.

By the end of 1866 advertisements in *The Times* show that Shoolbred and Co of Tottenham Court Road; J. Harvey and Son of Ludgate Hill; Hitchcock, Williams and Co of St Paul's

Churchyard; Debenham and Freebody of Cavendish Square; and Marshall and Snelgrove of Oxford Street closed at 2pm on Saturdays. However, Swan and Edgar of Regent Street closed at 6pm every evening, including Saturday in winter, and 7pm in summer. Some of these were recent converts to the half-holiday; for example, Marshall and Snelgrove only began in July and they were a firm then employing 700 people.[10]

In July the Duchess of Sutherland held a drawing-room meeting as a result of which 1,400 ladies pledged themselves not to shop after 2pm on Saturdays—possibly this influenced Marshall and Snelgrove.[11] A soiré in St James's Hall in November 1869 brought a 'well-dressed' company to hear a choir of 300 and listen to Anthony Trollope, under the chairmanship of Mr Morley, MP, but the best that could be reported was that, where it was not possible to adopt the 2pm closing the hours had been shortened.[12]

By the annual meeting of the association in 1872 the chairman, Mr W. C. Jay of Regent Street, having referred to his apprentice days when the drapery assistant belonged to the hardest worked class in the country, said of the association's work that 'thanks to the calm and judicious manner in which it had gone to work, the state of affairs he had alluded to was materially altered, and that he believed that in a very short time all the business houses in London would close at 2pm on Saturdays'.[13] It seems that his vision was limited to the West End for elsewhere in London the picture showed little, if any, improvement then, or in the years ahead.

In September 1872, just over four months after Mr Jay's statement, the South London Drapers' Association was formed to shorten hours. Its 250 members agreed to close at 8pm each evening. In two weeks only twenty were honouring the agreement and the movement collapsed.[14] At the annual meeting of the Early Closing Association in 1878 it was stated that there were many districts of London where early closing did not operate, and that in the East End and other districts many shops were open until 10 or 11pm for five days of the week and until midnight on Saturday.[15] By the next year the report referred to the erroneous and injurious impression prevailing that the work of the association was completed. At this meeting a letter was read from Gladstone, then prime minister, regretting that he was too busy to give the association active support but adding, 'I am very sensible of the value of the principle of early closing applied within the limits of what is practicable'.[16] The qualifying words typify the unwillingness of the statesman and of the association to go beyond exhortation and persuasion. It was axiomatic that the individual shopkeeper was free to run his business as he deemed best, however much other individuals, especially his assistants, might suffer as a result. The association, like many other groups of people and many individuals, had complete faith in the inevitability of gradualness. So Earl Cairns, a former chancellor, the chairman at the annual meeting in 1882, claimed that nearly all the wholesale houses and many of the retail ones gave a Saturday half-holiday and that much had been done, although much remained to be done, to shorten hours.[17]

Canon Farrar, notable ecclesiastic and schoolmaster, once well-remembered for his school story *Eric*, at the same meeting stated that probably 100,000 assistants in London worked twelve, fourteen or sixteen hours a day, without, apparently, seeing that he was already admitting that forty years of voluntary effort had not touched the core of the evil. By now the choir of former years had given place to brass bands, composed of young employees of Shoolbred's and Marshall and Snelgrove's stores. Did the performers, or those who enjoyed the gaiety they contributed to the proceedings, realise how far from typical were their conditions of service?

The Times on 22 January 1883 gave a fourth leader of nearly a column to comment on a recent report of the Early Closing Association in which the results of forty years of work were reviewed. Unfortunately the paper accepted the self-satisfied estimate of its work which the association gave. *The Times* says:

The contrast shown between the state of things when the association was founded and that which now prevails is very marked.
Both in London and in the provinces the early closing movement
has been making good progress, and although much still remains
to be done, though shops in some districts and in some departments of business are still kept open far beyond reasonable hours
yet a general improvement has been brought about, and a sensible
impression made upon the main evil, which the association was
formed to combat.[18]

It adds, 'A Saturday half-holiday, beginning at 2 o'clock, has
become an ordinary trade rule'.

Such statements show that the leader-writer knew only his
West End and cannot have bothered to read *The Times* itself
very carefully or he would have known that on 19 January it had
reported Mr E. Clarke, QC, MP, as saying that owing to their late
working hours shop-assistants were debarred from evening
classes; while Mr T. Sutherst, president of the Shop Hours'
Labour League, claimed that 'the present system of long hours is
injurious alike to shopkeepers and assistants, and is an evil that
demands speedy reform'.[19]

To return to the leading article of 22 January we find the
opinion expressed that, 'the early closing movement has so far
spread that the shops which have refused hitherto to adopt it will
soon find themselves driven to it. If they hang back, they must
submit to see their best shop hands seeking service elsewhere.'
This ignores the fact that most shop-assistants were only too glad
to obtain, or keep, a job whatever the conditions and the fact that
those who could be classed as 'the best' were a very small
minority. With a final flourish *The Times* declared that the battle
was almost won, and 'with a wave of public opinion to help him
on, the whole thing would be done speedily enough'.

An interesting commentary on the leader comes in a letter
from Charles Steinity of Camberwell, which *The Times* printed
on 25 January. The writer, acting at the request of 'a Christian
association', had tried in the previous summer to obtain early
closing on one day a week among the businesses employing

'young females' in Camberwell and Peckham. He secured a written pledge from the 'female heads of 5,000 families' not to shop after a certain hour. As a result, in the upper part of Camberwell—Denmark Hill, Camberwell Green, and Church Street—all the drapers agreed to close and kept their promise, but out of forty drapers etc in Rye Lane and Peckham High Street thirty-nine gave the promise to close but broke it because one of the smallest firms refused to give it.[20]

In May 1884 James A. Stacey, the secretary of the Early Closing Association, asked *The Times* to insert a short appeal to ladies to shop early. He believed that earlier appeals of a similar kind had been effective and he referred to an increasing number of Ladies' Early Closing Associations. He says that tradesmen frequently say to the association's canvassers, 'Get the people to shop early, and we shall close early'.[21] A special appeal is made to the wives of working men to buy their goods at an early hour. One wonders how many of these ladies would see *The Times*!

The same faith in the willingness of the customer to discipline himself, or herself, was expressed by the Bishop of Bedford when presiding at a meeting called by the Early Closing Association in Limehouse Town Hall in 1885. He first made the startling suggestion that to remedy the evil of late hours, 'the shop employees could combine and stand up for their rights and privileges by refusing to work late any longer. That might mean a strike, and he was not sure it would not be just and praiseworthy.' Then his courage failed and he turned quickly from notions so foreign to the supporters of the association to add, 'A better remedy, however, would be for the purchasing classes to abstain from shopping late'.[22]

By the middle of 1885 the association was admitting that only a minority of the shops in London were accepting the Saturday half-holiday. It considered that perhaps the worst thoroughfare in London for late Saturday closing ran from London Bridge through the borough of Walworth and Camberwell to Peckham. Yet it claimed that even here the majority of assistants were in shops that closed between 2pm and 5pm. It was very anxious to anticipate the growing demands that legislation should be sought to enforce earlier closing so it added: 'The multitude of small shops which struggle into existence year by year perpetuate for a time the late closing system, and make the progress of the movement less apparent than it is in reality. This should be borne in mind by those who repeat the many wild and random statements sometimes heard in support of an appeal to Parliament to enforce early closing.'

At the same time the support which the association continued to receive from those in high society was emphasised by receipt of a letter expressing the support of the Prince of Wales for the objects for which the association stood.[23]

This refusal to face the prospect of legislation had been one of the reasons for the comparative ineffectiveness of the association for a number of years. In 1871 the association had had little to report except that its help had been sought by a number of towns in the country, and in the following year it noted 'that a cry for legislation on the subject of early closing had been raised in the north, paralysing the good feeling which led employers to make concessions'.[24] This illustrates one of the reasons for the apathy of the assistants to the work of the association—it was all too obviously an employers' society. Further evidence of this growing demand for legislation came in 1874 when a weekly journal, *Capital and Labour*, reported: 'An agitation commencing in the north and extending to the metropolis, has been going forward for some time past with a view to obtaining an Act of Parliament which shall legislate the hours of labour in shops.' The association was asked to co-operate but its reaction was to discount the necessity for legislation or the likelihood of its effectiveness. It admitted that a case could be made out for limiting by law the hours of women and children but the difficulty found by women in obtaining employment made this an unattractive solution. It emphatically stated that legislation which aimed at fixing the hours when shops should close would be 'an unconstitutional intereference with the liberty of the subject'.[25]

A very different opinion was voiced in a study entitled *The State in Relation to Labour* which was published in 1882. The author, Dr W. Stanley Jevons, FRS, does not give much space to the shopworker but what he does say is very significant. In a chapter on the Factory Acts he writes,

> An important but hitherto little regarded kind of industry is that of men, women and young persons employed in retail shops and warehouses. When the work done is simply that of trade, as distinguished from manufacture, the State has hitherto held entirely aloof. The distinction is clearly an artificial one in many cases; the making up of pounds of sugar and the packing of goods is clearly a manual operation, or sometimes a machine operation, identical with much that is done in factories. Grocers' assistants, too, are frequently employed in grinding coffee, chopping loaf sugar, mixing teas, and the like. As a shopman or woman seldom sits down during the hours of work, the labour is exhausting in the long run. In the character of the work itself there is no reason why it should not be regulated as much as various handicrafts. The anomaly of the distinction drawn by the law is strongly marked in the case of some establishments where persons employed upstairs under the Factory and Workshop Act are brought downstairs to assist in the shop as soon as the legal hour has struck upon the clock.

From this the author assumes

> that the hours of shop-assistants' labour remain unregulated from regard to the convenience of the public, or else from regard to the profits of the employers. But the interests of the employers have not been allowed to stand in the way of the creation of the Factory Acts. It seems, then, that it is the public necessity of convenience which keeps shops open to ten or twelve o'clock at night, and obliges shop-assistants to labour, in many cases, from fourteen to eighteen, or even nineteen hours in the twenty-four.

Dr Jevons said that the existence of many early closing associations showed the discontent that was felt. He believed that in some areas considerable success had been achieved but that in many poor localities the hours were still very long. His conclusion is that 'only a strong spirit of trade unionism, or else the abstention of the public, or, in the last resort, legislative interference, can effect early closing'.

Dr Jevons is more realistic than the Early Closing Association when he assigns to social and industrial habits the pattern of hours which the association claimed, in part, to be the result of its work. Better-class shops closed earlier because their customers dined between 6pm and 7pm and, 'owing to our laissez-faire system of moral legislation, ladies especially are obliged to retire from the streets about that time'. But the workers were returning home from work between 5.30pm and 7pm and were ready, if not compelled, to shop then.

We are reminded of the prevailing conditions of housing and life generally for so many in the towns when Dr Jevons makes the only real qualification he can find of the wisdom of legislation. He says, 'Some doubt may arise as to whether the brightly-lighted streets of a poor neighbourhood do not really form the promenade ground of those who have few pleasures to relieve the dull monotonous round of a laborious life. To those who live in crowded dirty lodgings, unsavoury streets may be a breathing-place, and the well-filled shop-windows the only available museum of science and art.' That one who had viewed the situation of the shopworkers so clear-sightedly should hesitate over the possibility that thousands of people should work appalling hours to provide a little relief in the drab life of other thousands is typical of that timorous Victorian attitude which preferred, if it could not ignore bad social conditions, to suggest palliatives rather than cures.[26]

Whether Dr Jevons's book played any part in changing the attitude of the Early Closing Association to legislation cannot be verified but certainly more of its members were seeing that reliance on the voluntary principle left the heart of the problem untouched. By 1886 Mr Stacey, the association's secretary, could tell the Select Committee of the House of Commons, which was considering the Shop Hours Regulation Bill, that the association was not opposed to any legislation but that it had never initiated or supported it. This indicated a cautious abandonment of the policy of previous years.[27] By 1889 the association was supporting the legislative efforts of Sir John Lubbock, whose work will be dealt with later. From this date the association, while not relaxing its efforts to secure its aims by voluntary agreement, was active in support of the attempts to obtain some legislative sanction for shorter hours.

The report of the association for 1889 recorded among the objects of the association, as amended in 1887, the intention 'To watch over and promote the interests of traders and their assistants, in matters requiring Municipal or Legislative control'. While the association could claim for the first time to have secured a general closing among drapers in East London at 2pm on Thursdays it had to report that hours of closing on other days, especially Saturdays, in all trades in many districts were now as late or sometimes later than at any time in the last fifteen or twenty years. This it accounted for by trade rivalries and 'one man' minorities and it admitted that little change was likely except through legislation. Details of the work attempted in different towns in the country illustrated the ebb and flow of the tide of success. The Norwich Association had been re-organised in 1888 and was one of the strongest provincial societies: one hundred shops closed at 2pm on Thursdays in summer. The Torquay Association, formed barely a year before, had 'died of inanition'. At Bradford a lot of time and money had been spent on the half-holiday movement but the opposition of a few had resulted in failure.[28]

The association's report for 1891 told the same story of gain —usually temporary—here, and loss there. In many areas of London it found that even if a 5pm closing had been agreed for a Wednesday or Thursday, 'there is no reduction, but rather an increase in many districts, of late closing on other days'. The report said 'it is lamentable that so great a necessity for the

Society's work should remain', and added, 'After fifty years' preaching and teaching (and the Society's cause has been warmly espoused in the pulpit and the press) the destruction of health and happiness, in many districts, is almost as great as ever'. Finally, the report stated, 'It is not public convenience which prevents the fuller emancipation of its victims, but the cheapness of human life—principally that of the shop girl'.[29]

One feels that at last the complacency of the Early Closing Association had been destroyed, but it had taken far too long. In its new, more realistic approach to the problem the association did not carry all its members. The more timid among its supporters and those who were belligerent for the cause of laissez-faire could not agree with the new policy of looking for legislative sanction for shorter hours. Some of these formed in December 1890 the South London Early Closing Association, 'to promote the early closing of shops by voluntary effort only'. This became, by November 1892, the Voluntary Early Closing Association under the presidency of Sir John Blundell Maple, who declared that 'the members of the association held that the man who wished to keep his shop open must not be compelled to close it at the dictates of any other individual', and that 'compulsory closing interfered with the liberty of the subject'. Sir John made it clear that he could no longer support the parent Early Closing Association because he considered that it had 'completely changed its policy'. He said that he was opposed to the compulsory closing of shops, especially when mines and factories were not closed by legislation. He claimed that the Voluntary Association 'sprang from the tenacity and loyalty of some of the old members of the board of management of the Early Closing Association to the original policy of that society in advocating the voluntary early closing of shops'.[30]

As more efforts were made to secure legislation to shorten shop hours the rivalry of these two early closing associations would be seen. Increasing support for legislative action would show that more people were aware that the easy optimism of the sixties was outdated. Yet the survival of that optimism was to prevent real reform for another twenty years.

CHAPTER FIVE

THE WORK OF SIR JOHN LUBBOCK, TO 1886

It was in 1871 that bank officials first obtained four statutory holidays—Easter Monday, Monday in Whitsun week, the first Monday in August, and the day after Christmas Day. The *Annual Register* for 1871, under the date 7 August which was the first such holiday, says it 'was generally observed throughout the country. The Government Offices in London remained open, but the warehouses and offices of public companies, the Royal Exchange, and Lloyd's were all closed, and many of the shops in the city. In Liverpool the day was observed as strictly as if it were Good Friday or Christmas Day.'[1]

The *Illustrated London News*, on its front page on 19 August, had a picture showing 'the crowded state of Margate Jetty on the gleesome occasion, as one boat-load of excursionists quickly followed another, taking the town pleasantly by storm'. Another illustration inside showed a medley of characters watching a keeper feed the animals at the Zoological Society's Gardens in

Regent's Park. In its description of the way the day was spent the magazine says : 'The name of Sir John Lubbock and the first Monday in August will henceforth be associated with pleasant recollections in the minds of the clerks of the bankers, brokers, merchants, and traders of the City.' It states that 'nearly all the retail shops in Cannon Street, the Poultry, and Cornhall were closed', but 'along the Strand, Piccadilly, Holborn, and Oxford Street, with few exceptions, the shops were open, and in Regent Street only twelve were shut up'. Even so the writer enthuses over the joys of the day variously spent by many released from work in the 'main factories' of 'the east end of the town', while 'several schools gave a whole holiday to the pupils'.[2]

Few people today remember Sir John Lubbock as the chief instigator of these holidays. Fewer still know anything of his unwearied advocacy of legislation to secure shorter hours for shopworkers. His biographer claims that one object which Sir John had in consenting to stand for election to Parliament to represent Maidstone as a Liberal was to serve the interests of small shopkeepers and shop-assistants.[3] Consequently, in 1871 he drafted a bill, in addition to the Bank Holiday Bill, which proposed to deal with shops on the lines of the existing factory legislation. He submitted it to his friend, Mr W. Rathbone, a member for Liverpool. His reply was non-committal and he felt that he did not know enough of the subject to judge whether a bill, rigidly fixing the number of hours when a shop could be open, was satisfactory. He felt there might be cases 'in which a relay of hands might be desirable, say in the mining districts'.[4] Whether this led Sir John to feel he must himself study the question more deeply we do not know, but it was not until April 1873 that he introduced a bill on the lines he had proposed in 1871. This proposed to extend to shops the provisions of the Workshops Acts of 1867-71. Shops would have to close at 2pm on one week-day each week. Women, apprentices under twenty-one and children were not to be employed on Good Friday or Christmas Day and were to have in addition four days or eight half-days as holidays in the year. The permitted ten-hour working day could be extended on market day to a fifteen-hour day by permission of the secretary of state.[5]

This bill was attacked by Mrs Millicent Garrett Fawcett, the wife of the statesman and economist and herself a writer on economic problems, on the grounds that it would endanger the employment of women. She regarded the measure as inspired by 'the old Trade Union spirit to drive women out of certain trades where their competition is inconvenient'. This fear that legislative protection for women would handicap them in the labour market was to hamper the struggle for legislation to safeguard workers in shops for a long time. *The Times* of 9 June 1873, which printed Mrs Fawcett's letter, gave a fourth leader of almost a column to comment on it. This does not support Mrs Fawcett. The writer points out that if everyone was good and wise laws would be unnecessary, and that

> if men and women were actually equal before the world, there would be no need for restraints upon female labour. But, as society is constituted, the assumed conditions can be looked for only in some far-distant future; and, until they are realised, it will still be necessary to protect the weak against the encroachments of the strong, and to regulate the extent and character of the protection by the incidents which each day's experience brings to light.[6]

A meeting at Norwich, convened and presided over by the mayor, Sir S. Brignold, passed a resolution condemning the bill on the grounds that it would press unjustly on the tradesmen, curtail the employment of women, and discourage the training of apprentices.[7] As the society most concerned with bettering conditions was, as we have seen, opposed to legislation it is not surprising to find vested interests having a free field in attacking the bill. As a result the bill was dropped and Sir John did not renew his efforts to get it passed for ten years.

In the summer of 1880 the shopkeepers themselves, in Manchester, declared that hours were too long and a general half-

F

holiday needed which 'could be brought about only by legislative action'.[8] In 1884 Liverpool tried to obtain better conditions by a local bill but it failed to get a second reading. It proposed that it should be unlawful in Liverpool for any shops 'to be open on Sundays for any period whatever, nor shall it be lawful for them to be open on any of the first five days of the week beyond the hour of eight o'clock in the evening or on Saturdays beyond ten o'clock in the evening'.[9]

Sir John Lubbock followed this up in the same year by a bill which had the support of, among others, Lord Randolph Churchill; this bill was more moderate than his previous one. It only proposed a limit of twelve hours a day on young persons (between the ages of thirteen and eighteen) working in shops. Even so it did not secure a second reading.[10]

A similar bill, which Sir John introduced in 1885, passed its second reading without a division but its opponents blocked further progress. Its sponsor felt that he had made headway in that Mr Hopwood, who led the opposition to it, preferred to use parliamentary procedure in order to prevent the bill reaching the committee stage rather than face the possibility of the House passing it.[11]

In January 1886 Sir John once more brought in a bill to limit the hours of young persons in shops to twelve a day. In moving the second reading on 18 February Sir John said that the Shop Hours' League (to be discussed later) had collected a lot of evidence of long hours and bad conditions, and he quoted some of the examples to the House. A girl of nineteen had been in a drapery business in Battersea for four and a half years and the hours had been 8.30am to 9.30pm for five days a week and 8.30 am to midnight on Saturdays. Another girl of the same age at a drapery business in King's Cross worked thirteen or thirteen and a half hours for five days a week and worked until midnight on Saturdays, often not leaving the shop until 12.30 or 1am on Sunday morning. Of these hours twenty or twenty-five minutes were allowed for dinner and fifteen minutes for other meals. The girl said, 'I am always thankful when Sunday comes; but I am never fit to go to a place of worship till night'.

A girl in a Camberwell shop, who began business life at fifteen and a half, said the usual hours were 8 or 8.30am till 9.30 or 10pm with 11.30 or midnight on Saturdays. No stated times were allowed for meals as the assistants were expected to eat as quickly as possible and hurry back to the counter. She was often unwell and suffered fainting fits from long standing, and pains in the feet and legs. A girl at Deptford gave her hours as 8am to 10pm for five days a week and 8am to midnight on Saturdays. Fifteen or twenty minutes were supposed to be allowed for each meal but assistants were often called away to serve. When she began her shop career she was in good health but she had to give up her job because she developed consumption. She said, 'I have never been able to get for a walk except on a Sunday, as no respectable girl cares to go out between 10 and 11 at night. After the fatigue and worry of the week I am so thoroughly worn out that my only thought is to rest on a Sunday.'

In commenting on these cases Sir John said: 'It is stated that probably one half of the drapers' assistants in London never enter a place of worship, and those who do are so drowsy that they can scarcely keep awake.' He claimed that the cases he had quoted were not exceptional. He gave figures to show the number of shops open to a late hour in various parts of London, and these included 200 out of 250 shops in Islington open until 9.30pm; 150 out of 200 at Hackney; 200 out of 250 at Hammersmith; 120 out of 175 at Bow; in Bermondsey 320 out of 400 were open until 10pm as was the case with 350 out of 450 at Lambeth, 140 out of 200 at Battersea, 120 out of 150 at Poplar, and 225 out of 300 at Stoke Newington; while 475 out of 600 in Whitechapel were open until 10.15. On Saturday a large proportion of shops kept open until midnight.

Sir John pointed out that these bad conditions were not peculiar to London—they were similar in Liverpool, in Brighton the hours were the same as London, Bristol had long hours, and in Chester, Derby, Huddersfield, Leeds and York the hours totalled about eighty a week. He pointed out that the bill introduced no new principle, 'it merely extends to shops that which is already the law in workshops'. He said that generally shopkeepers wanted shorter hours, but 'in almost every case the arrangements for early closing have been rendered negatory by the action of some very small minority among the shopkeepers'.

In the debate Professor Thorold Rogers, Liberal member for Southwark, supported the general principle of the bill but thought the circumstances of London south of the Thames differed from the West End. Late hours were essential in some areas. He suggested a Select Committee of the House to examine the whole question. Others supported this suggestion and when Sir John agreed the bill was read a second time and referred to a Select Committee of the House.[12]

Sir John Lubbock and Mr Thorold Rogers were among the eight members of the committee which examined twelve shop-assistants, twenty-one representatives of various trade and early closing associations, a similar number of traders called by supporters of the bill, and fourteen traders called by different members of the committee, five factory-inspectors and two medical men. The report and record of evidence submitted to the committee covered 340 foolscap pages and was issued on 18 May 1886. The committee had worked quickly and thoroughly.

The committee was satisfied that 'the practice of keeping open shops until a late hour in the evening prevails extensively', especially on Saturday. It found that in many places the hours of shop-assistants were eighty-four or eighty-five hours a week, and it felt that such long hours, especially in crowded and ill-ventilated premises, must be injurious to health, especially for girls. It noted, as we have seen Dr Jevons did in 1882, an evasion of the existing workshop regulations, for it pointed out that in shops with workrooms attached, young persons 'who could not be employed in the latter beyond that statutory hours of the Factory and Workshop Act are called upon to serve after their tasks in the workrooms have been finished'. The committee pointed out that apprentices and young people often worked for some time preparing the shop before it opened and packing goods away after it closed.

The report stated that, 'The great majority of witnesses expressed their opinion that though voluntary action had effected much improvement, little could be expected from it in the poorer neighbourhoods, and that nothing short of legislation would be effective'. The committee, therefore, strongly supported the bill but added, 'A widespread desire has also been expressed by grown-up persons employed in shops, that in some way their labours also may be limited by law; and your Committee believe that employers are not indisposed as a rule to such limitation, provided that it takes the form of general early closing of shops'. It supports this belief by saying that it has evidence that in many places the desire of a majority of shopkeepers to close early has been frustrated by the refusal of the few, and that large shops keep open longer than they would wish for fear of the competition of smaller shops which keep open longer. The committee made the comment that, although the bill exempted public houses and refreshment houses, it considered the work in these to be at least as fatiguing and injurious as in shops.[13]

In giving evidence before the committee Robert Dixon, speaking for the Manchester and District Grocery Trade Defence Association, said that his employees in two shops worked from 8am to 9pm from Monday to Thursday, from 8am to 10pm on Fridays and only finished at 11pm on Saturdays. But as compensation for these hours they had every fourth Monday off, with pay, and one week's holiday in summer with pay. This arrangement for some holiday time was something unknown to most assistants.[14]

Edwin Hide, speaking for the Portsmouth Chamber of Commerce, claimed to run a business on the lines of Marshall and Snelgrove, only smaller. His shop opened at 8.30am but male apprentices began work at 7am and had from 8-9am for breakfast; female apprentices began at 7.35am and were also free from 8-9am. All the assistants, he claimed, were away from the shop ten minutes after it closed in the evening. Between 10.45 and 11am the assistants went into the house for bread and butter and cheese; there was half an hour for dinner between 1 and 2pm; and twenty-five or thirty minutes off for tea. Closing times were: October to March inclusive, 7pm; April, May and September, 7.30pm; June, July, August, 8pm. On Saturday the business closed at 5pm—the only one to do so in the town for twenty years, until the previous summer. The assistants had Bank Holidays, the Coronation holiday, and, after six months' service, a week's holiday with pay, or, after ten months' service, two weeks' holiday with pay, together with two clear days for travelling. The apprentices became improvers or assistants at seventeen or eighteen and were then paid £12-£20 a year; this had risen to £25-£40 a year by the age of twenty-three or twenty-four. The witness claimed that the Portsmouth Chamber of Commerce favoured closing by legislation because a small minority of owners compelled the majority to keep open later than they thought necessary.[15] Obviously this was a business, probably because of its size and class of trade, in which conditions were far better than in the average small shop. By contrast the Portsmouth grocers closed at 8pm on four nights and found it difficult to do so by 9.30pm on Friday and 10.30pm on Saturday.[16]

In the same way when Frank Debenham, of Debenham and Freebody of London, gave evidence the picture was very different from the average of over eighty hours a week work which the committee had found. He said the hours in his shop were sixty-four or sixty-five a week. Some assistants started at 7am but the shop did not open until 8.30am and closed at 6pm for six months of the year and at 7pm for the other six months. On Saturday the shop closed at 2pm. All Bank Holidays were observed and the staff had a week's holiday a year. The apprentices did not pay a premium, as was the usual practice, and assistants from the age of twenty-one to thirty or thirty-five were paid £20-80 a year, together with board and lodging, while buyers and more experienced workers were paid from £100 to £400 or £500 a year.[17]

A very different type of employer was Thomas Layman, who told the committee that he had a draper's shop in Southwark, a jeweller's, draper's and pawnbroker's shop in Newington, another pawnbroker's shop in Bermondsey and one in the Old Kent Road. He employed forty assistants, some of whom worked a nine-hour day, with an hour out for dinner, some a ten-hour day, and some a twelve-hour day with thirteen or fourteen hours on Saturday. All had the Bank Holidays free and those who worked the twelve-hour day had one free day every four weeks or part of a day weekly or several days at long intervals. All this seems so open to variation that one imagines the employees to have been very much at the mercy of their employer's whim. His attitude to his workers is seen, too, when he told the committee that his employees could have as much extra holiday as they liked at their own cost, adding, 'I wish to impress very positively the advantage of the arrangement of their taking holidays at their own cost, because it cultivates in them that spirit of independence and self-reliance which it is so desirable that they should cultivate, and unless they do a little at their own cost they would never cultivate it at all'. We are not told how far any succeeded in taking holidays to cultivate this virtue on wages of 15s or 16s a week for those under eighteen, if working outdoors, or 12s indoors, or 5s a week with board and lodging; or, if over eighteen, outdoor men earned 30s to 40s and indoor men 20s to 25s.[18]

Evidence given to the committee showed great differences in hours and conditions in London. Charles Walton, with tea-dealers' shops in east and north London, opened at 8.30am and closed at 8pm on four nights, with 9.30pm closing on Friday and nearly midnight on Saturday. George Swaffield, a tailor's assistant in Hackney, said that in his first shop, when aged fifteen, his hours had been 7.45am to 9 or 9.30pm on four days, with 9.45pm closing on Friday and midnight, or half an hour later, on Saturday. Later, in Shoreditch, where his hours had been less than those of the other assistants, because he was a cutter, he had worked from 9am to 9pm on four days, with 9.30 closing on Friday and 11pm on Saturday. A hatter, with three shops in the Finsbury Park, Euston Road area, opened from 8am to 10pm six days a week. Mark Blow, a fruiterer and green-grocer, with shops in Peckham and Bermondsey, said that his hours were those of his trade generally, namely 7am or 7.30am to 11pm or midnight on five days a week and on Saturday closing half an hour or an hour after midnight. He added, 'I know a shop that never closed till 2 o'clock'. The vice-chairman of the Trades-man's Association for the Harrow Road district, himself a grocer, said that in his district the usual hours were 7.30am to 9.30pm or 10pm for five days and midnight, or after, on Saturday. William Alderson, an invalid at thirty-one on account of long hours, who had been an assistant in the tea, wine and grocery trade, said that in his first shop, in the Baker Street area, he had worked from 7.15am to 8.30pm or 9.15pm four days a week, with a closing hour of 9pm or 9.30pm on Friday and midnight on Saturday.[19]

A shopkeeper in Hoxton Street (which he admitted was one of the poorest streets in London) with three shops in Shoreditch, selling tin goods, kettles, saucepans etc, said that all his shops were small, with two boys in each, managed by his family, and the shops opened at 8.30am and closed at 10.15pm and 11.45pm on Saturdays. These were the usual hours for the neighbour-hood, he said, and he knew one fishmonger who opened for fifteen hours a day for five days, sixteen hours on Saturdays, and twelve hours on Sundays.[20]

To move a little farther out in the London area, to Woolwich, a milliner and fancy draper gave the general closing hours for the district as 9pm or 9.30pm on four days, 5pm on one day, and 10pm or 11pm on Saturdays. That he could say that a mid-week closing at 5pm was general in his neighbourhood indicated an unusual position in the London area at this time. He added that very few assistants under thirteen were paid at all and that from sixteen to eighteen they received £10 to £20 a year, and from twenty to twenty-five, £20 to £50 or £60 a year.[21]

The evidence of Frank Debenham has shown a different picture for the big West End shops confirmed by A. J. Marshall of Marshall & Snelgrove.[22] John Barker of Kensington, with over 400 assistants in his drapery, furnishing and grocery store, closed at 6.30pm in the winter and only as late as 8pm for two months at the height of the season, with a 2pm Saturday closing all the year. He said all the small shops were open until 9pm or 9.30pm for five nights a week with a 10pm or midnight closing on Saturdays.[23] Thomas Lilley, of Lilley & Skinner, chairman of the Boot and Shoe and Leather Trades Association and chairman of Paddington Early Closing Association said that with small shopkeepers the voluntary effort was useless and a bill to close all shops at 8pm five days a week and 10pm Saturdays was needed.

Looking at other parts of the country we have the following glimpses of varying conditions. From Lancashire a manager of a grocer's shop in Stalybridge who was the secretary of the local Early Closing Association said that the general hours in the town were 8am to 9pm, Monday to Thursday, with closing at 10pm on Friday and 11pm on Saturday. He said that the assistants were not away from a shop until nearly half an hour after closing time. From his knowledge of the town this witness was able to give the committee some information which can be substantiated from other sources. He said that there were several co-operative stores in Stalybridge and their hours of closing were 8pm on Monday, Wednesday, Thursday, Friday, 7pm on Saturday, and a half-holiday on Tuesday. Of the other shops only the grocers, drapers and boot shops had a half-holiday. It would seem that co-operative shops could have shorter hours because they had not the same fear as other shops that their customers would shop elsewhere—the customers were not likely to sacrifice dividend. At the same time, what happened in Stalybridge made nonsense of the claim, often advanced, that it was necessary to keep open late to meet the needs of the working-class home. For the local mills closed at 5pm or 5.30pm for five days a week and at 1pm on Saturdays.[24]

From Newcastle-on-Tyne a draper with three shops gave the hours worked as ten and a half for five days a week and fourteen on Saturday, justifying the long hours on Saturday by saying that people came from the villages to shop as it was market day (it seems strange that villagers did not want to start the journey home before 11pm or midnight!). He said the best shops closed at 9pm on Saturday and a few at 7pm on the other nights of the week. There was no half-holiday observed and he makes the surprising statement that the shopkeepers did not close on Bank Holidays.[25]

A witness from Sheffield gave the general hours of closing as two nights at 8pm, three at 7pm, one at 10pm or 11pm, but in summer the 7pm became 8pm. He was a draper and general furnisher employing fifty assistants, who began work at 8.30am (except for an early dusting party which came at 7.30am) and finished at 7pm for five nights a week, and at 10pm on Saturdays. He mentioned that two shops, in what he termed the finer drapery trade and furnishing, closed at 5pm on Saturdays. His own shop and nearly all the Sheffield shops observed the Bank Holidays and some of his assistants had twelve days' holiday beside. He gave an interesting peep into the conditions for those of his assistants who lived in. He said that they could throw the dining-room, shopwalkers' room, and library into one room for music, recreation and an occasional dance, and added, 'I am glad to say that they have temperance meetings, prayer meetings, a Bible class, and a week ago I took the chair while the Venerable Archdeacon Blakeney, the Vicar of Sheffield, gave us a Bible reading of an interesting kind'. His apprentices received no wages but paid a premium and lived in. Boys, whom he called cash boys, who had just passed the standard that enabled them to go to work, were paid 3s 6d, 4s or 5s a week. Assistants aged twenty to twenty-five were paid £20 to £50 a year.[26]

A similar picture to Sheffield was given for Bolton, by an accountant who was the secretary of the local early closing association, except that many shops closed at 1pm on Wednesdays. He added, however, that this was not nearly as many as the 400 shops that had closed at 1pm twelve years before.[27]

A better state of affairs was indicated for the small market towns of North Lancashire, Cumberland and Westmorland by the factory-inspector for that area. He said that shop hours were only long for one day a week, a day which was sometimes in the middle of the week. He gave the hours of better-class shops in Preston as 8am to 6pm, with one day 8pm. He does not say what hours the other shops kept. Blackburn he described as about the same; Barrow was 6am to 6pm with one day 8pm; while he said Carlisle and Penrith were not so long.[28]

A witness with outfitters' shops in Yarmouth and Lowestoft gave his hours as fourteen for five days and sixteen on Saturdays. Apparently other shops closed earlier, for he said some of his customers were employed in other shops and came to him when their own shops were closed. He said, unlike many of the witnesses, who favoured the proposed bill, that if the bill became law he would be ruined.[29]

Many witnesses were emphatic that although the Early Closing Associations had achieved some good, but limited, results, legislation was needed, otherwise a few selfish individuals could bar progress. They not only supported the bill under investigation but suggested a law to compel a fixed closing hour daily. A number favoured an 8pm closing for five days and a 10pm on Saturdays. It should be noted that these hours envisaged a much longer working week for shop-assistants than for factory workers.[30]

The secretary of the East London Early Closing Association suggested a seventy-two hour week and a Thursday 5pm closing. He said that assistants would be prepared to work longer hours on Saturdays if they could have the 5pm Thursday closing.[31] He believed that East End shops needed to stay open until 10pm on Saturdays.

Several witnesses pointed out the necessity of stopping Sunday trading. One said: 'If we have to shut up our shops at 10 o'clock on Saturday night, and the people can get what they want on Sunday morning, you will, in that case, inflict very great hardship upon us.' Especially as there were no Jews in his neighbourhood (Hoxton Street, London), he could not understand the tolerant attitude of the police in allowing Sunday trading to continue.[32] A similar point was made by a Bermondsey draper who felt that the fines for Sunday trading should be increased from half a crown to £1.[33]

Some witnesses opposed the bill and any form of legislation. The gentleman who had justified making his assistants take their holidays without pay was one, because all legislative interference with mercantile life sapped independence, and he did not think that the purpose of legislation should be to protect young people from overwork. In fact he objected to all factory legislation.[34] He found a supporter for much of his attitude in Frederick Shoolbred of the well-known furniture and general store in Tottenham Court Road, employing 700 assistants. He said he was opposed to all legislative interference, even with the labour of the young, and admitted that he agreed with laissez-faire. He thought that the Early Closing Association had made great improvements. Later in his evidence he seemed to weaken in this attitude, under questioning, for he admitted that he would favour legislation to shut all shops at fixed times. He may have been influenced by the fact, which he had stated earlier, that the smaller shops in his area kept open much longer than his shop, which kept similar hours to the big stores, with a 2pm Saturday closing. In fact one of the committee, Mr Thorold Rogers, referred to Shoolbred's as a household word for a well-conducted business.[35]

From Sheffield the witness already mentioned opposed legislation, unless it was an act fixing compulsory hours for all shops,

because, he said, 'I do not think that the young people suffer
under the present arrangements; they are not hardly worked;
there is very considerable leisure at certain seasons of the year,
and more or less leisure through the day at all seasons'.[36]

The president of the Portsmouth and South Hants Grocers'
Association opposed legislation, but if there had to be any it
should apply to all.[37] A revealing statement was made by a witness
from the Old Kent Road, London, who opposed any legislation
because he thought that voluntary effort would succeed. This
although he said he employed his assistants in a drapery shop
for eighty-three hours a week, and 'I have joined every early
closing movement that has been brought forward during the last
twenty-six years'.[38]

J. B. Maple of the upholsterers' firm in Tottenham Court
Road, London, told the committee that the bill 'is a direct and
harassing infringement of the liberty of the subject'. How little
he understood the situation outside his own business was shown
when he continued: 'It is a well-known fact that employees
generally have been better treated of recent years than at any
previous period, with regard to hours of work and domestic
surroundings; the half-holiday system obtaining in a great number of the provincial towns and London.' Although he opposed
legislation he found nothing illogical in his query, 'Why is not
the law enforced in England, and all shops closed on Sundays?'
Was it dislike for the co-operative movement which made him
say it would be better if the co-operative shops worked longer
hours in order to cater better for the needs of their members?[39]

It will be worth while to compare the evidence given to the
committee by Thomas Sutherst, the chairman of the Shop Hours'
League, and James Austin Stacey, the secretary of the Early
Closing Association. Sutherst admitted that he framed the bill,
although he would have preferred a bill limiting the hours of all
shopworkers. He made two important points when he said that
bad conditions often prevailed where businesses were started in
a small way, prospered, the premises were then enlarged but the

rooms were kept low and crowded; and when he pointed out that he estimated that half the shop-assistants were under twenty-one years of age, especially in the large towns. He considered that in London and several provincial towns seventy-five to ninety per cent of employers favoured compulsory closing; a minority thwarted any voluntary action, including the half-holiday idea. He pointed out that the Early Closing Association had existed for forty years but its chief success had been in fashionable and highly respectable neighbourhoods because the customers there did not wish to shop late. He hoped the committee would not confuse these successes with the success of the persuasive system generally, 'because it is well known that in the large centres, in the populous centres of industry throughout the country, and more particularly in the metropolis, the hours are almost, if not quite, as long as they were a great many years ago, and with the best intentions these early closing societies have undoubtedly failed to effect a permanent improvement in the hours of labour'.

After pointing out that, by legislation, the artisan had had his hours reduced to fifty-six a week, he said, 'I do not find any fault with the Early Closing Association except that in my opinion it might have adopted the principle of legislation some considerable time ago'. He made an important point when he said that the shop-assistant was handicapped in trying to form a trade union to further his own interests because he needed 'a character' when seeking a new post, and this was not obtainable if he showed any independence, while the artisan could get a job without a reference. Then, most shop-assistants were too young to understand the importance of united action. In his estimation public opinion was apathetic and if shops were open, whatever the hour, people would enter them even though they knew the employees were being overworked.[40]

Mr Stacey proved a most unsatisfactory witness. The committee was evidently puzzled by him. It is often not clear whether he is expressing his own views or those of his association. He claimed that his association had passed no resolution about the bill under consideration but had permitted him to appear to give evidence. He said that his association was not opposed to any legislation but it had never initiated any or supported any. He admitted that in the past the association had been against the idea of legislation and under cross-examination he hedged as to whether it would really support any now. He indicated that a number of the subscribers of the association had recently changed their minds and now favoured legislation. He claimed that five or six associations had sprung up in the previous twenty years to promote legislation to shorten shop hours, but after making a brief stir they had disappeared while his association, supporting the voluntary effort, had flourished.[41]

The first six months of 1886 during which the bill was under consideration by Parliament were naturally times of activity in press and public meeting by supporters and opponents of the measure. An outstanding meeting was held at the Mansion House, London, on 1 April. It was called by opponents of the bill and attended by shopkeepers from all over England who were expected to agree to a resolution condemning it. Instead, after a speech by Sir John Lubbock, those attending the meeting passed, by a large majority, a resolution

> That, though preferring a limit of 72 hours per week instead of 12 hours per day, this meeting heartily accepts Sir John Lubbock's Bill, which would undoubtedly confer great benefit on young persons engaged in shops, and earnestly prays Parliament to go further and to add a clause enacting a compulsory general closing at 8pm on four days of the week and 10 o'clock on Saturdays, which would confer an inestimable benefit on the whole shop-keeping community and relieve them from the intolerably long hours from which they now suffer.[42]

The significance of this was not lost on the Early Closing Association: its secretary, whose evidence has just been considered, testified to another select committee of the House of Commons in 1895 that it was this Mansion House meeting, which he called a landmark in the history of early closing, together with inquiries that the association made itself as a result of the meeting, which led the association to realise that it had been out of touch with the real opinion of traders on the matter of legislation.[43]

Mr Maple, as would be expected, championed the cause of the small trader who did not like the bill. In a letter to *The Times* he challenged the claim of Sir John Lubbock that the Mansion House meeting represented the views of the small trader. He said that as the meeting was held at 3pm very few small traders could be there. The really small shopkeepers held a meeting, on the evening of the Mansion House meeting, in Camden Town and passed a resolution 'That this meeting of shopkeepers of St Pancras condemns the Shop Hours' Regulation Bill as being an unworkable measure, and pledges itself to take such steps as may be possible to prevent its third reading'. Maple had canvassed the traders of South St Pancras himself and he claimed that they were seven to one against 'any legislative interference with the liberties of the subject'.[44]

The council of the London Chamber of Commerce opposed the bill at a meeting held on 8 April for two reasons: 'Firstly, that, in their opinion, sufficient cause has not yet been shown for legislative interference with the ordinary course of business. Secondly, that the passing of the Bill would have the detrimental effect of decreasing the employment of juvenile labour.'[45] Was this a conscious or unintentional euphemism prompted by the council's desire to be able to employ the cheap labour of youth for as long as its members desired?

The bill, as amended (with the consent of Sir John Lubbock) by the select committee to read that no young person was to be employed more than seventy-four hours, including mealtimes, in one week, instead of the original twelve hours a day, was made law on 25 June 1886. It did not apply to a shop run solely by the members of one family, it was to come into operation on 1 November 1886 and to continue until 31 December 1888 and 'the end of the then next session of Parliament and no longer'.[46]

Parliament had at last admitted that the conditions of work of young people in shops was its concern. Beyond that it was certainly not prepared to go, for it gave no consideration to a bill which Sir John Lubbock, with the support of Mr Barry, one of the select committee, introduced in August 1886 to try to give effect to the suggestions that had been made for legislation to fix definite closing hours. By it all shops were to close not later than 10pm on Saturdays and 8pm on other days and the local authority, at the request of two-thirds of the occupiers of shops, could enforce an earlier closing on one day a week provided it was not before 2pm. Also in the bill an attempt was made to deal with the abuse of the law with regard to Sunday trading to which witnesses before the select committee had made reference. It was proposed to increase the penalty for breaking the act prohibiting Sunday trading from 5s to £1.[47]

Although this bill was unsuccessful—its supporters can hardly have expected success so soon—at least one old gentleman must have felt, before the year was out, that England was rapidly going downhill. There had appeared in *The Times,* on 5 January 1886, a letter signed 'Ancient Citizen' which expressed thoughts as familiar to us now as then. The writer said: 'The present generation work not as their fathers before them, to whom Saturday was the most hardworked day of the week. Now the young men of this time think more of football, bicycle, and the cricket field than the advancement of their country's commerce.'[48]

CHAPTER SIX

THOMAS SUTHERST AND THE SHOP HOURS' LABOUR LEAGUE

On the afternoon of Sunday, 25 September 1881 a meeting was held at Pentonville convened by a new body called the Shop-Assistants' Twelve Hours' Labour League. The chairman explained that they met on Sunday because there was no other aay on which shop-assistants could meet. He claimed that the majority of shop-assistants worked ninety-eight hours a week and that their wages worked out at less than 9d an hour. Speakers who followed supported this statement, one saying that women engaged in a shop in Tottenham Court Road worked ninety hours a week, were unprovided with any seats and had insufficient time to take meals. The meeting passed a resolution registering its conviction that legislation was essential to secure a twelve-hour working day.[1]

In the following year the same league held a meeting in Trafalgar Square.[2] This time it evidently relied for support on those assistants from the West End or City that had a half-holiday for it chose the afternoon of Saturday, 29 April. The chairman on this occasion claimed that there were 320,000 shop-assistants in London and the majority of these worked for sixteen or seventeen hours daily. The secretary of the league, Morley Alderson, read letters of support from the Duke of Albany and J. C. Collins, MP, and the latter promised to support the aims of the league in the House of Commons. The league had now dropped the words 'Twelve Hours' from its title and its aim had become a ten-hour day. It was reported in May that the Earl of Shaftesbury had written to the secretary to express 'a very deep and true sympathy' with the aims of the league, and that many Members of Parliament had suggested that the assistants form a strong trade union. In Liverpool a public meeting had urged the need for legislation to secure a ten-hour day.[3]

On Sunday, 26 November the body, now known as the Shop Hours' Labour League, held a demonstration of shopkeepers and assistants in the Royal Albert Hall, attended by 10,000 people.[4] Lord Brabazon presided and the secretary reported a membership of 6,000. The chairman said that he believed that the government were under some promise to Lord Stanhope to introduce a bill to protect women and children in certain establishments. The president of the league, T. Sutherst, moved a resolution demanding legislation to secure a 5pm closing in all shops on one day of the week.

This league not only stimulated the Early Closing Association to greater efforts in the 1880s but roused the assistants and the public to the need for legislation as they had not been roused before. The driving force in the league was its president, Thomas Sutherst, a barrister. He collected a mass of evidence on the actual conditions prevailing in the shops and in 1884 he published some of his findings under the title *Death and Disease Behind the Counter*. It was a yellow-covered book, about five inches by seven, containing some 280 pages of information.[5] Its startling title was to be justified, even if people ignored the contents, by several parliamentary committees, one of which has already been studied.

In his preface, dated May 1884, Sutherst said that about two years before he presided at a Hyde Park meeting held to protest against conditions in the shops. As a result of that experience, he helped to start the league. On the basis of figures which he had collected from all over England he estimated that the majority of shop-assistants worked from seventy-five to ninety hours a week. He suggested that of the majority one-quarter worked ninety hours; one-half eighty hours; and one-quarter seventy-five hours. There was a minority in the high-class shops, who worked less than the seventy-five hours. He outlined the evils of standing for these long hours in bad air, with time only for hurried meals.

Then he instanced a number of cases to illustrate conditions. A man of forty years of age, then the manager of a large establishment, had worked for twenty-six years in shops in Liverpool, Manchester, Birmingham and London but would not be able to stand the life much longer. He had never worked less than eighty hours a week, and usually it has been ninety. He said there were very few old men in the shops and he thought the majority were under twenty-one. He had worked hard for the early closing movement only to see the selfishness of a few cause the abandonment of the half-holiday after it had been obtained. This man said he felt fit only for bed on Sundays. Another shopworker, a young man of twenty-one, who had been employed in the drapery trade since he was fourteen, and whose hours were 7am to 9pm with 11pm on Saturdays, said, 'I used to have a Sunday school class, but now I neither have the time nor the inclination for such things'.

Typical of the fact that conditions were worse in London and the big industrial areas than the small country towns was the case of a man of twenty who was a draper at King's Cross and whose hours were 7 to 9.30 with 10.30 on Saturday; he stated: 'I was at Falmouth four years, and the hours there were reasonable, and so were mealtimes.'

At Lewes a draper's assistant, a woman of twenty-three, reported her hours as 8am to 8pm for five days a week and 10.30pm on Saturday. An hour was allowed for dinner and half an hour for tea.

In Sheffield a man of thirty-two had had three situations— all in leading shops in the city—and the hours for four days a week had been 8 to 8.30 or 9 to 9.15. On Saturdays the hours of closing had varied from 9pm to 11pm. In all cases half an hour had been allowed for dinner and the same for tea. There was at present a 5pm closing on Thursday but he did not expect this to continue as only three of the original fifteen drapers who had brought this about now observed it.

An ironmonger's assistant of twenty-five at Leicester had, when apprenticed, worked for five days from 7.30 to 7 with 8 o'clock closing on Saturday. He had had an hour's break for breakfast, an hour for dinner, and a quarter of an hour for tea —but on Saturdays, market days, only quarter of an hour was allowed for dinner. In his present position he worked from 8 to 7 on all days of the week. He no longer lived in and was allowed an hour for dinner and quarter of an hour for tea. There was no early closing but half the assistants were away on alternate Thursday afternoons.

A bootmaker's assistant at Southsea, Hampshire, said that in his first position his hours had been 8.30 to 9.30 with midnight on Saturdays; and that now they were 8 to 9.30 with 11pm on Saturdays.

From Bury, Lancashire, comes the report of a draper whose hours were from an unspecified time in the morning to 9pm, with 11 or midnight on Saturday, but for the last six months there had been a weekly half-holiday on Tuesdays.

Typical of the lack of uniformity in hours from trade to trade and place to place was a Manchester draper who began work at 6.30am in summer and 7am in winter, whereas in Newcastle-on-Tyne a boot salesman did not begin work until 9am on any day in the year. Here a clothier's assistant began work at 8.45am but finished at 7pm every day while a grocer gave his hours as 8am to 8pm, Monday to Friday; and 8am to 10pm on Saturday. This

Newcastle grocer told Sutherst that he felt that the Christian churches should acknowledge and act on the belief that this life is given us for enjoyment. These grocery hours contrast with those prevailing in St Mary Cray, Kent, which were 7.30am to 10pm for five days a week and a midnight closing on Saturday. A Newcastle boot salesman gave his hours as 9am to 8pm for four days with 9pm closing on Friday and 11pm on Saturday. There were good conditions, compared with most places, in Southport where drapery and millinery assistants began at 9am and finished at 7pm, with a 5pm closing on Saturdays, and enjoyed sixteen days' paid annual holiday, in addition to Christmas Day, Good Friday and the Bank Holidays.

In his book Sutherst outlined a bill which he had drafted to remedy the bad conditions of which he had given ample evidence. He felt that a simple extension of the Factory and Workshops Act to cover shops would be the best solution. His bill contained provisions for the proper ventilation and cleanliness of shops, prohibited the employment of children under ten years of age, and limited the hours of employment of those between ten and thirteen to $4\frac{1}{2}$ hours a day, between 8am and 8pm. Young persons, that is those of thirteen to eighteen, who had obtained a certificate of proficiency in reading, writing and arithmetic, were to be employed not more than twelve hours a day and these times of work were to fall between 6am and 8pm on five days of the week and 6am to 10pm on one day. On one day of the week all employees—adults and young persons—were to have a seven hour day only, between 6am and 5pm. All employees were to have $1\frac{1}{2}$ hours for meals, except on the half-holiday, when one hour was allowed. No child or young person could be employed on Sunday. The measure was to apply to every shop or warehouse with one or more assistants, in all places in England and Wales with over 20,000 inhabitants, and it was to be enforced by inspectors.

Sutherst explained his exemption of smaller places by saying, 'it is well known that in small towns and rural districts there is no necessity whatever to interfere, except probably on the ground of sanitary inspection'. With reference to Sunday opening he wrote: 'I should very much have liked to have seen a prospect of stopping Sunday trading altogether, as I am quite sure there is no necessity whatever for business to be conducted on the Sabbath day. I am well aware that it does not prevail to a large extent, but in London and other large towns hundreds of drapers', tailors', butchers' and other shops are open until mid-day on Sunday, without any excuse whatever except the desire to make money, by pandering to the thoughtlessness of persons who might, without difficulty, make their purchases on Saturday.'[6] This statement illustrates again the fact that those who advocated a Sunday free from unnecessary work were often among the chief supporters of shorter weekday working hours and early closing.

The year before Sutherst's book was published the Shop Hours' Labour League stimulated activity which *The Times* felt it necessary to report more frequently. For example, it gave a third of a column on 19 January 1883 to a 'largely attended' public meeting at Bridge-House Hotel, London Bridge, called by the 'South London Thursday Five o'clock Closing Association', to advocate a 5pm closure on Thursdays. This meeting was supported by the two Members of Parliament for Lambeth together with Sir John Lubbock and Thomas Sutherst. The chairman of the meeting, another Member of Parliament, said that, 'connected as he was with the largest set of evening educational classes in London, he knew that comparatively few of the students who attended them were shop-assistants', because the long hours of work debarred them.[7]

The Times gave half a column to reporting an 'East End demonstration', organised by the Shop Hours' Labour League, at the Standard Theatre, Shoreditch, on a Sunday afternoon in February 1883.[8] A number of eminent men wrote to Sutherst supporting the meeting, including the Right Honourable W. E. Forster, MP, whose name will always be linked with the Education Act of 1870, who had resigned from the post of Irish

Secretary in the Gladstone government the previous year over the release of Parnell and others from prison. He stated that, 'The very fact of your meeting being held on Sunday is a proof of the great need for shorter hours.' Lord Claude Hamilton, who presided at the meeting, was forthright in demanding legislation to fix shop hours.

Sutherst and the league supported Lubbock's bills in 1884 and 1885. Meetings were organised and the London Trades' Council unanimously resolved to back the 1885 bill, while expressing regret that it did not go far enough. The council called 'upon all people to have due regard for their fellow workers employed in shops, by obtaining the articles necessary for general subsistence at the earliest possible time'.[9] In June the league organised a demonstration in support of the bill at the Prince's Hall, Piccadilly. It was something of a triumph for Sutherst to have secured Lord Bramwell as chairman of the meeting for he was known as a great supporter of individual independence and an opponent of government interference. He indicated that here was a case needing legislation to protect the weak and defenceless, although he did not favour legislation compelling a man to close his shop.[10] Thus, by aiming at a more limited objective than the league desired, Sir John Lubbock secured the support of men who thought like Lord Bramwell. These included Cardinal Manning and the Bishop of London, who sat on the platform at the meeting.

During 1885 there was published some interesting correspondence which had passed between Sutherst and the Earl of Wemyss, the chairman of the Liberty and Property Defence League, following a request to the Earl of Wemyss to become a patron of the Shop Hours' Labour League.[11] The Liberty and Property Defence League stood for 'self-Help versus State Help', and 'for resisting overlegislation, for maintaining freedom of contract, and for advocating individualism as opposed to socialism, entirely irrespective of party politics'. It considered the legislation of the previous fifteen years indicated 'a general movement towards

State-socialism'. Branches of the society existed in Liverpool, Manchester, Leeds, Sheffield, Nottingham, York, Bristol, Plymouth and Bournemouth. Naturally, therefore, in his first letter the Earl of Wemyss stated that, while prepared to encourage early closing by united action, he was opposed to state interference. He had accepted the idea that 'early closing on Saturdays has become very general, not only in the Metropolis but throughout the Kingdom', and he stated that this 'was brought about by public opinion, and kindly feeling and arrangement between employers and employed; and if by the same means like results on other week-days can be obtained, no one will rejoice more than I'.

He suggested that if employees wanted shorter hours they should obtain them by trade union effort. This preference for trade union action rather than legislation is interesting and one wonders whether it was prompted by the knowledge that no effective trade union for shop-assistants existed and that therefore any interference with the freedom of the employer to do as he liked by that method was very remote. In a later letter, it having been pointed out to him that Lubbock's bill applied only to those under eighteen years of age, the Earl of Wemyss declared his approval of that bill but wanted to know whether the Shop Hours' Labour League approved the Liverpool Bill of 1884 and whether the league was pledged not to seek for further state interference with adults. Only if assured on these points could he become a patron of the league.

Sutherst, in his answer, said that the league did not approve of, or support, the Liverpool Bill and that its only immediate legislative aims were to see Lubbock's bill made law. Yet he made it clear that if this did not happen he could give no pledge as to the league's future policy. It is not surprising, therefore, that the Earl of Wemyss declined to become a patron, confirmed in his belief that the league contemplated legislative interference with adults.

CHAPTER SEVEN

1887-1900: A LEGISLATIVE VERSUS VOLUNTARY SOLUTION

By the late 1880s and early 1890s the struggle to obtain shorter hours for the shopworkers was becoming more sharply defined. The complacency of the Early Closing Association was ending and it was committed to supporting legislative action, even if it was not sure what the limits of that action should be. The Shop Hours' Labour League was urging an even more rigid control by Parliament than the Early Closing Association would favour. The trade unions were emerging to demand legislation, although they would not be able to claim the active backing of all the assistants. Over against these were ranged those who objected to legislation, either because they did not believe it to be the right way to achieve desirable ends or because they did not think the ends desirable. Among these objectors there would soon be the members of the new Voluntary Early Closing Association.

Early in 1887 Sir John Lubbock introduced a bill[1] to close all shops at 8pm on five days a week and at 10pm on Saturdays. By it, on the application of at least two thirds of the shopkeepers, a local authority could fix an earlier closing hour on one day a week provided the hour was not earlier than 2pm. The bill also substituted the penalty of £1 for the 5s fine in existence for Sunday trading. The cause of laissez-faire found a new advocate in Lord Charles Beresford, who admitted that the bill would benefit 55,000 shop-assistants (his estimate of their numbers), but who also believed that this was more than offset by the fact that it would inconvenience 'half a million of persons, ruin thousands of small tradesmen, and, I believe, inflict a severe hardship on large numbers of the general public'.[2]

Sir John, having no success with this bill, re-introduced it in 1888 but it was lost again by 280 to 97 on the second reading.[3] However, the act of 1886 (see the end of Chapter 4) was renewed in 1888 until 31 December 1889.[4] Sir John Lubbock seems to have felt that he would have to modify his objectives and so, in 1889, the bill he introduced aimed only at establishing a half-holiday by local option.[5] This brought a protest from Mr James Platt of St Martin's Lane, London, an old opponent, who wrote : 'It is another phase of the tyranny of the majority, the sacrificing or putting aside the right of the minority, and should be resisted to the utmost. It simply means the ruin of the smaller shop-keepers.'[6] He claimed that in many districts the shopkeepers closed at 6pm on one day a week and that they were willing to close as early as circumstances would allow. He added, 'I for one object most strongly to these attempts at compulsory early closing, and think the time has come to let these people understand that free Englishmen will not be interfered with in this way'.

He was answered by Mr J. A. Stacey, the secretary of the Early Closing Association, who made the shrewd thrust that 'both he and Mr Maple [his fellow-opponent of the bill] were the great twins in joining the Saturday half-holiday last of all among the principal firms of the metropolis'.[7] One wonders how disinterested was Mr Platt's championship of freedom and on what grounds he claimed to represent the small shopkeeper. Mr

Stacey added that the bill had been introduced at the request
of the Early Closing Association—another sign that the society
had now committed itself to supporting legislative action.

Another opponent of the bill, Mr J. D. Power, used a most
curious argument when he wrote to *The Times* from the
Temple, London, to say that if all the London shop people who
now worked a six day week 'were suddenly to become unemployed for one afternoon in the week there would instantly be
found, probably by an ingenious company promoter, some form
of labour by which they could earn a certain amount during that
afternoon, and by this amount the shop wages would inevitably
be reduced'.[8]

In 1890, no success having come in 1889, Sir John Lubbock,
with the support of the Early Closing Association, put the Half-
Holiday Bill forward again.[9] Surprisingly, we find Mr Blundell
Maple sponsoring a bill in the same year. He had so far opposed
all legislation, claiming in 1888, when leading the attack on
Lubbock's bill, that 'a great many Gladstonian Liberals' had
promised to support him by voting against 'this piece of faddist
and fanatical legislation'.[10] Probably he felt Sir John's Half-
Holiday Bill was likely to succeed unless he could forestall it
with a measure that would seem to serve the desired end without all the interference with the freedom of the employer that
Sir John's bill implied. At any rate he introduced a bill to provide
that every shopkeeper should, on one working day a week
selected by himself, give his assistants a half-holiday. Such half-
holidays were to begin not later than 4pm and could only be
claimed after three months' service with the employer. The
employer would have to give three days' notice to the employee
of the day on which he, or she, was to have the holiday. Each
shop would have to keep a register showing the days of holiday
for each assistant and the latter would have to sign this each week
as evidence of having had the holiday. Shops closing regularly
before 4pm on one day a week were exempt from the act. With
no arrangement for adequate inspection—an idea that Mr Maple,

and those who thought like him, had always strenuously opposed —the bill seems to have been drafted to provide every possible loophole for the unscrupulous employer.[11]

Lack of provision for inspection had already meant that the act of 1886 was often ignored. As early as the autumn of 1887 the secretary of a body called the Shop Hours' Regulation Act Committee was writing to *The Times* to remind its readers of the provisions of the act and to state that the committee would prosecute breaches of the law.[12] By 1890 Mr Thomas Sutherst, the president of the Shop Hours' League, stated that the act 'is flagrantly violated, as there are thousands of boys and girls in the metropolis working from 80 to 100 hours a week'.[13]

Neither Lubbock's bill nor Maple's bill met with any success. There was a deputation, organised by the Early Closing Association on behalf of Lubbock's bill, which met the Home Secretary, Mr H. Matthew, in March.[14] Introduced by Sir John Lubbock it consisted not only of a number of members of parliament but of representatives of a number of London boroughs together with those from Oxford, Birmingham, Hull, Lincoln, Newcastle-on-Tyne, Reading, Bristol, Cardiff, Bedford, Edinburgh, Glasgow, Dundee, Liverpool, Manchester, Norwich and Margate. It stated that a petition in favour of the principles of the bill had been presented to the House of Commons which had been signed by most of the bishops, 200 of the London clergy, almost all the London priests, and 300 London Nonconformist ministers. The bill had the support of the London Trades Council and similar councils in other places. The deputation hoped to secure government support for the bill but was unsuccessful.

After another unsuccessful attempt by Sir John Lubbock, in 1891, to secure the passing of his bill the year 1892 saw greater parliamentary activity. Not only did Lubbock and Maple renew their efforts of 1890 but Mr A. D. Provand, a Manchester merchant who represented Glasgow, introduced a bill, as he had done in 1890, to make permanent the Shop Hours' Act of 1886, which had been renewed annually since 1889, with the addition of a clause bringing women within the scope of the act and a clause providing for the appointment of inspectors. In the preamble the bill pointed out that by a Factory Act of 1844 the hours of women had been limited to sixty a week whereas this bill now permitted seventy-four hours a week, less mealtime periods.[15]

In the debate on the bill it was pointed out that the Early Closing Association, which four years before had been hostile to any restriction being put on the hours of women workers, had circulated every working women's club or society which it knew and the replies had shown a substantial testimony in favour of such a measure while no hostile criticism of the bill had been made. This seemed to dispose of the argument advanced against the bill to the effect that women would be thrown out of work if it became law. Mr Baumann, who seconded the moving of the second reading of the bill, produced evidence to show that work in shops was more exhausting to women than work in mills, emphasising that the variety of muscular action required in the factory was less trying than the long hours of standing in the shop. In dealing with one type of objection to the bill Mr Bauman used words which have not become entirely outdated when he said: 'There is another class of political philosophers opposed to legislation of this kind, who style themselves Individualists, the forlorn and fading remnant of an exploded school. I am an Individualist, but I am in favour of protecting, and not oppressing the individual. In the struggle between the feeble and the strong, it is liberty which oppresses; it is the law which enfranchises and protects.'

Mr Sydney Gedge, a solicitor and Conservative member for Stockport, put forward the old laissez-faire claim that women should be free to sell their labour as they wished without restraint of the law but introduced a new ingenious twist, which one feels was expressed with his tongue in his cheek, when he proposed as an amendment that 'This House declines to further interfere with the hours of labour of adult women until women have the constitutional means of expressing their opinion by the "Parliamentary Franchise".'

Mr A. B. Winterbotham, member for Bristol, who spoke as an employer of women and on behalf of many in Bristol and the towns of the West, claimed that the better class of shopkeeper desired such legislation and dealt in a forthright way with the argument that to appoint inspectors was to violate the sanctity of the shop; he said that if a shop was open eighty or ninety hours a week, 'the sanctity deserves to be violated'. Mr J. R. Kelly, member for Camberwell North, made the obvious statement, which equally obviously had been shown for many years to be beyond achievement: 'Induce the public to shop early, and there will be no necessity whatever for the Bill.' Of government speakers Mr H. Matthew, still home secretary, was opposed to the bill and Mr A. J. Balfour, the First Lord of the Treasury, wanted an inquiry. In the end the bill passed its second reading by 175 to 152 and was sent to a select committee of the House.

The committee of eighteen, including Sir John Lubbock, Mr Blundell Maple, and Mr Provand, made its report on 16 June 1892.[16] It suggested that the Shop Hours' Act of 1886 be made permanent, but it could not agree that it should apply to adult women. The committee stated that many witnesses who advocated its extention to women admitted that they hoped thereby to make general early closing inevitable. It agreed that the act of 1886 had in general not been enforced and that it was to a great extent unknown and so it proposed that inspectors should be appointed by the local authorities to see that the act was observed.

Very interesting evidence was given to the committee by Mr Frank Hardern, president of the Oldham Co-operative Society. It bears out the point, suggested before in this book, that the co-operative societies had often closed their shops earlier than their competitors, without inconveniencing their customers. Mr Hardern gave the hours of his own and twelve other societies in the neighbourhood as fifty-eight at the maximum and fifty-five at the minimum. The Stratford, London, society employed its assistants sixty hours and the Woolwich society 60½ hours. All these figures excluded mealtimes. Some Northumberland societies had adopted a forty-eight hour week. Shops in many cases closed in the dinner hour—an interesting innovation which was not to be followed generally until World War I. The witness claimed that the co-operative shops in the north of England really instituted the half-holiday in many places thirty years before. In more detail the hours of the co-operative shops in Oldham were given as 8am until 8pm on Monday, Wednesday, Thursday; 8am to noon on Tuesday; 8am to 9pm on Friday, and on Saturday 8am to 6pm. The average hours of other shops in Oldham were given as 8am to 8pm, with no mid-day closing and no half-holiday, for three days a week, with a closing time for many of 9pm or 10pm on Thursday, Friday and Saturday. Some were open until midnight on Saturday. The point was made that the spinners in Oldham—and most of the co-operative members were spinners—ceased work at 5.30pm and so late shopping was unnecessary.

Alderman John Barker, JP, who had given evidence in 1886, told the committee that he considered legislation for men and women was required. In his Kensington store he now employed over 1,000 people, men and women in about equal proportion. Including the one and a half hours allowed for dinner and tea the women were employed for 62½ hours a week and the men another three hours a week over this. In making both estimates three and a half hours a week had been included to cover the time spent in clearing up the shop after closing hours, and in some cases this time had not been needed. The shop closed at 7pm on five nights a week and at 2pm on Saturday. It opened at 7.30am but the women assistants did not come on duty until 8.30. In addition to Bank Holidays all assistants, after twelve months' service, had two weeks' holiday with pay. Mr Barker said that the small shops in Kensington shut at 9pm on five days a week and at 11pm on Saturday. He said that in many London shops women worked seventy-four hours or more a week. Typical of the story repeated in so many places was the information Mr Barker gave that some years ago he and the Rev Carr Glynn went to the small drapers of Kensington and all agreed to close at 8pm on five days a week and at 9pm on Saturday. This was observed for a few months and then one draper kept open longer than the agreed hours and soon all were back to the old times.

Mr William Johnson, General Secretary of the National Union of Shop-Assistants, said that the worst hours he knew were those in the Manchester grocery trade, which corroborates the account of the previous year in *Shop Life Reform*. He instanced, as the worst case, a grocer's boy of sixteen who worked $15\frac{1}{2}$ hours for five days a week, sixteen hours on Saturday and five hours on Sunday. He also did two hours a week overtime. He had a half-day on Christmas Day, Good Friday and general holidays together with one whole day a year on full pay. His wage was £1 a month. The witness said that in the centre of Manchester some only worked a fifty-hour week with a half holiday on Saturday. Outside the centre the average hours worked were eighty.

An inspector of factories, Mr J. B. Lakeman, who had given evidence in 1886, considered that little change had taken place in four years and he said that the act of 1886 was a dead letter. Mr D. C. Cornes had been employed by the Early Closing Association to investigate shop hours in various parts of London. He told the committee that he considered the Old Kent Road representative of London, except for the West End and Edgware Road, and for the Old Kent Road he gave the total hours that various types of shop were open in the week as follows: bakers, 91, butchers, 86 to 91, china and glass shops, and boot and shoe shops, 80 to 87, stationery and watchmakers and furniture dealers' shops, 80 to 86, provision dealers, 86 to 92, confectioners, 86 to 91, hatters, 78 to 87, ironmongers, 80 to 90, oil and colour dealers, 86 to 88, and tailors, 75 to 81. He considered that the selfishness and apathy of the public were the cause of such long hours continuing.

Miss Gertrude King, secretary of the Society for Promoting

H

the Employment of Women, told the committee that her society opposed the bill under consideration because it feared it would throw women out of employment. This view was the opposite of that put forward in the debate on the second reading, based on the investigation of the Early Closing Association and repeated before the committee by Mr Cornes.

Parliament followed the recommendations of the committee and the only new feature of importance in the act of 1892 was the provision that county or borough councils might appoint inspectors to enforce the act.[17] But this was a permissive clause and by 16 March 1893 the under-secretary for the Home Department, Mr H. Gladstone, reported to the House of Commons that returns to date showed that four counties had appointed inspectors; forty-five had not; four had the matter under consideration; seven had not replied; thirty-five boroughs had appointed forty-eight inspectors; one hundred and ninety-one had not; fifteen had the matter under consideration; and sixty had not replied.[18]

A few days later the House of Commons was made to face the subject of shop hours once more when Sir John Lubbock moved the following resolution, which was agreed to after a debate, in which most of the old arguments in favour of, and in opposition to, legislation were voiced. The resolution read:

> That, in the opinion of this House, the excessive and unnecessarily long hours of labour in shops are injurious to the comfort, health and well-being of all concerned; and that it is desirable to give the local authorities such powers as may be necessary to enable them to carry out the general wishes of the shopkeeping community with reference to the hours of closing.[19]

We need not follow the speeches of Sir John Lubbock and Sir J. Blundell Maple but some points by others who took part in the debate are worth noting. Mr G. C. T. Bartley in seconding the resolution used words which had a refreshing note for those times; he said 'that the object of labour was to secure life, happiness, and independence', and that life was not simply intended for labour.

Mr H. H. Asquith, the home secretary, said that the government was permitting a free vote on the resolution with which he, personally, was in favour. He admitted that the act of 1886, made permanent the previous year, had not produced any serious result, partly because adults and young people worked together. Therefore, he concluded: 'If you are to deal with the question comprehensively and effectively, you must ignore distinctions and look to the employees as a whole.' He agreed that voluntary effort had proved a powerful force in attaining a Saturday half-holiday in London and the larger provincial towns but it was insufficient to win complete success. He gave a personal experience of the failure of the voluntary system when he mentioned that a year or two ago the City of London hairdressers had agreed to close at 4pm on Saturday. In a few months he saw a notice in one shop that the hour was changed to 6pm and on inquiry he was told that one large employer had refused to agree to the 4pm arrangement and so the others had abandoned it. He said that it was not possible to organise the public to refrain from shopping when shops were open. 'I have therefore come to the conclusion long ago that this is one of those cases in which voluntary combined action is ineffective to the end in view.' When Mr Asquith mentioned that some argued that Parliament ought not to interfere with the voluntary action of adults, the Opposition applauded. But he went on to say that he did not accept the view, factory legislation had indirectly limited the hours of adult labour and he could see no difference between indirect and direct interference.

Evidently Mr Asquith's views were not those of his cabinet colleagues for the country was going to have to wait until Mr Asquith was prime minister before anything really satisfactory was done.

Dr Farquharson, a medical man who represented West Aberdeenshire, supported the resolution, saying: 'The House has heard about black slaves in Uganda, but there were white slaves to be found here; and these poor people had, moreover, no trade union to protect them.' Many years before, Lord Shaftesbury had been called the Wilberforce of the Whites because of his work for the 'factory slaves' of England—it seems amazing that this much more obvious slavery was still so largely ignored and has been so easily forgotten. Having passed the resolution, which in itself did nothing, Parliament seems to have been content to forget about the subject—after all, the white slaves did not parade their slavery; they did not in the majority of cases protest against it; and many people had a vested interest in allowing it to go on.

Sir John Lubbock did not abandon his efforts and in February 1895 the House of Commons gave a second reading to his Shops (Early Closing) Bill and sent it to a select committee.[20] This procedure seems amazing except that, as the passing of the resolution of 1893 shows, a majority of members of the House of Commons felt that something should be done but were afraid to do anything. What conclusion it was expected would emerge from the investigation, other than the conclusions of 1886 and 1892, probably no member who voted for another consideration by a select committee could have said. Some may have hoped that the situation would be shown to have improved. If so they were to be disappointed. From the point of view of tracing the story of shop conditions another committee's work is valuable for it brings out evidence difficult or impossible to obtain in any other way.

The committee set up in February 1895, which reported in May, was presided over by Sir John Lubbock and included not only Sir Blundell Maple but Dr Farquharson, who had referred to 'white slaves' in 1893.[21] The committee asked Mr J. A. Stacey, who had been the secretary of the Early Closing Association for nearly twenty years, if there had been any change in the general situation since 1886. His reply was, 'Not in respect to the ordinary hours of closing, but there has been an advance in a mid-weekly closing; that is, progress has been made with the closing at five or two on Wednesdays or Thursdays.' On the other hand he considered that in many parts of London conditions were slightly worse than in 1875. Significantly he admitted that, while over the past fifty years the Early Closing Association had spent £100,000 and while the half-holiday had been secured for the wholesale trade and for the principal retail trade houses, 'in regard to the poorer districts we made no appreciable impression'. He made the point that Great Britain was lagging behind her overseas connections in that Victoria, New South Wales and New Zealand already had more drastic legislation in operation than was contemplated in this bill. He considered the hours in London in general to be 81-2 a week if there were a 5pm closing on one day a week; if not the hours were eighty-five or more.

Mr Henry Horsman, who represented the Manchester branch of the National Union of Shop-Assistants—the branch from which the National Union developed—said the branch had 600 members in Manchester, where it had been estimated that there were at least 5,000 shop-assistants. He said a Wednesday half-holiday was fairly general in Manchester but a number of shops worked later on Tuesday and Thursday as a result. The chairman quoted the report of the Corporation of Manchester inspector under the Shop Hours' Act as stating that in the centre of the city tobacconists and confectioners were open ninety hours and more. In contrast, in the Manchester co-operative shops the hours worked were 56-8 a week. This tallies with the information given to the 1892 committee for the Oldham area. The biographer of the Right Honourable F. W. Jowett of Bradford claims that he originated shorter hours for the whole co-operative movement in 1889.[22] However, the co-operative shops were, in some places, working shorter hours before that date. In Bradford, the change came when Mr Jowett, finding that assistants worked until 10pm on Friday and as late on Saturday, although they had a half-holiday, tabled a resolution at the half-yearly meeting to reduce the hours drastically and this was carried by a large majority. In those last few words no doubt lies the clue to the difference between the success of the co-operative movement in reducing hours, and the failure of the various efforts to persuade the general public to abstain from shopping at private traders who kept long hours. There were always the people who lacked public spirit or disliked anything that to them savoured of interference with their supposed right to do as they liked. In the case of the private trader the opportunity to gain the custom of these people induced him to keep open. In the co-operative movement these people were in the minority at a meeting which decided policy and therefore could be ignored, for it can be presumed that few of them left the society on the score that their liberty was infringed.

Some interesting information was given to the committee by Mr E. Day, the secretary of the West Yorkshire Federated Chamber of Trade, representing sixteen tradesmen's associations in Yorkshire, all in favour of the bill.[23] The facts which he provided for places he knew were as follows. At Batley there was early closing on Wednesday—hour not given—for all except confectioners, tobacconists and pawnbrokers, but the latter closed early on Thursday. The hours for the other days were 8am to 8pm on Monday, Tuesday and Thursday, 9pm Friday, 11pm Saturday. At Brighouse shops closed at 1pm on Tuesday but small shops and sweetshops and tobacconists kept open. Cleckheaton and Heckmondwike shops closed at 1pm on Wednesday except for the ironmongers, confectioners and butchers in the former and the confectioners and pork butchers in the latter, where also the ironmongers kept open until 5pm. All this, and what follows, illustrates the illogical situation that still usually prevailed. At Dewsbury there was almost complete closing at 1pm on Wednesday and on other days the hours were 8am to 9pm for four days and 11pm on Saturday. In Halifax some shops in the main streets closed at 1pm on Monday, most at 1pm on Thursday. In the side streets and suburbs the half-holiday was not generally observed or, where shops closed at 1pm, they reopened at 6pm. In Sheffield there was a 2pm closing on Thursday except for the grocers, some of whom closed at 2pm and others at 4pm. On other days, the hours were in general 8.30am to 8pm. In Bradford the grocers, ironmongers and pawnbrokers were the only shops to have a half-holiday and the average hours worked a week were seventy, with one and a quarter hours a day off for meals. Leeds had no general early closing and in Huddersfield a number of shops did not close when the others closed at 1pm. At Hebden Bridge there was a fairly general half-holiday and the hours on other days were 8am to 8pm with 9pm on Friday and 10pm on Saturday. At Sowerby Bridge and Shipley the half-holiday was not observed by the small tradesmen. Wakefield had tried a 1pm closing but it had failed and now the hour was 4pm, but not all shops observed it. The hours on other days were 8am to 7 or 7.30pm, with 11pm on Saturday.

Mr A. Vicar of Bolton gave the hours there as 8.30am to 8.30pm on Monday and Friday, 8am to 8pm Tuesday and Thursday, 8am to 1pm Wednesday, 8am to 10pm on Saturday in the middle of the town but 10.30 or 11pm elsewhere.[24] Once again the co-operative shops had shorter hours, for they closed half an hour earlier on two nights a week and an hour earlier on Saturday, but these were not such good hours as we have noticed elsewhere. Another witness from Bolton, however, said that the drapers opened at 7.30am and did not shut until nearly midnight on Saturday.

The secretary of the Liverpool Grocery and Provision Dealers' Association put grocers' hours at 8am to 10pm on four days a week, with 11pm closing on Friday and midnight, or after, on Saturday. William Greenwood, chairman of the Northern Federation of Hairdressers, with 750 members, chiefly around Manchester, said that hairdressers' hours were eighty or ninety a week, including Sunday. He made the interesting point that any prosecution for Sunday work often failed because the act of Charles II prohibited a person following his legitimate occupation on Sunday and so a magistrate could not fine a factory worker who shaved customers on Sunday.[25]

The vice-president of the Metropolitan Grocers' and Provision

Dealers' Association, Mr Henry Cushen, who was the chairman of a firm of oil and colourmen with eighty shops in the Metropolitan area and forty years' experience of the trade, put the anti-legislation point of view with vigour, saying: 'I object, on behalf of the Metropolitan Grocers' and Provision Dealers' Association, to any experimental interference with adult labour in the retail trades of the Metropolis, especially in view of the fact that Sir John Lubbock's Shops' Early Closing Bill is an entirely novel proposed departure from the usual liberty of male adults to make contracts for their own labour.'[26] That Mr Cushen represented, quite apart from his official capacity, that body of traders where interpretation of liberty was licence to please themselves and ignore everyone else, is shown by the fact that after praising the work of the Early Closing Association and its rival, he told the committee that he was not prepared to co-operate with the Early Closing Association or with anyone but that he would close his shop when he thought he would. It is not surprising to read that the hours of closing of his own shops, which opened at 8am, were 9pm on the first three nights of the week; 4 or 5pm on Thursday; 9, 10 or 10.30pm on Friday; and 11pm or midnight on Saturday.

Those sending petitions in support of the bill as listed by the committee included the Archbishop of Canterbury, the Bishop of London, several other bishops, 500 London Anglican clergy and Nonconformist ministers, Cardinal Manning, many Roman Catholic priests, 500 matrons and nurses of London hospitals and over 300 London medical men.[27] The committee recommended the passing of the bill but that was the end of it—no further time was found for it by the House. Yet Parliament could find time to amend the act of 1892—as it had done in 1893. On neither occasion was the amendment such as to touch the liberty of the shopkeeper to impose what conditions he liked upon his adult assistants—that is why time could be found by the government for safe amendments but not for private measures that challenged still widely held notions of miscalled freedom. The amendment in 1893 allowed any expenses under the 1892 act to be met from the rates and the 1895 amendment imposed a fine of forty shillings for not exhibiting the notice required by the act of 1892 showing the hours young people were allowed to work.[28]

In 1896 there was published volume VII of Charles Booth's valuable study, *Life and Labour of the People in London,* in which detailed information is given of shopping conditions.[29] With regard to actual hours worked all the information given illustrates the now familiar picture. After referring to the work of the two rival early closing associations, the writer concluded that 'since 1890 more voluntary improvement has been made in London than in any other five years'. He added, 'But the latest reports of the younger society show the great difficulty it finds in carrying out its principle. It is very easy for a few determined opponents to make the reduced hours impossible'; concluding, 'it may be that the limits of voluntary action have been reached for the present.' He stated that although in wholesale and high-class businesses 'hours have been greatly reduced', yet 'in low-class trade, and especially in the suburbs, long hours are still the rule, and any improvement gained has been slight'. He favoured, whether by compulsory or voluntary means, the fixing of a total figure for the hours to be worked in a week, leaving it to the individual shop-owner to decide for his own business how this figure should be spread over the week. He suggested, in this connection, that 'a shop which claimed to be first-class might be limited to fifty-five hours, second-class sixty or sixty-five, and third-class seventy', adding, 'a limit to the prolongation of work after the doors are shut would seem to be within the scope of trade union or even individual action'. One feels that, apart from the invidious suggestion of attempting to classify shops, the proposal failed to face up to the facts of the situation, which must have been known to one with the information at his disposal that Booth possessed. He must have known that no trade union had anything like the support necessary to fulfil the function he would allot to it and 'individual action' in the case of the shop-assistant was almost an impossibility in any effective way.

The Fabian Tract Number 80, published in 1897, to which reference was made in the last chapter, gave figures for co-operative society shops which supported earlier evidence that they so often pioneered earlier closing hours in a neighbourhood. It quoted a report for 1895 of the Women's Co-operative Guild which stated that '530 women and girls were employed as shop-assistants by 104 societies and that the average hours worked were 53¾ per week; 38, or seven per cent, worked 48 hours or less per week; 179, or 34 per cent, from 49 to 53 hours; 240, or 45 per cent, from 53 to 57 hours; 59, or 11 per cent, from 57 to 60 hours; and 14, or 3 per cent, 60 hours or upwards'. The author of the tract gave the hours worked by men in co-operative shops as averaging, in 1896, 53.6 a week. He concluded: 'If working people, who are generally credited with a passion for late shopping, can get their business done in these comparatively short hours, there is no reason why any shop should remain open longer. But so long as a greedy shopkeeper is willing to cater for the person at the margin of humanity, it will be impossible to trust simply to the moralisation of the customer.'

The writer of the tract mentioned that the returns under the Shop Hours' Act of 1892 showed that only ten full-time inspectors had been appointed in Great Britain, of which number five were for England and Wales. He pointed out that the only other law affecting shop-assistants was the Truck Act of 1892 which gave inspectors the right to enter a shop.

Early in 1896 Sir John Lubbock introduced his Shops (Early Closing) Bill once more but he met with no greater success than on earlier occasions.[30] The bill, however, led to considerable correspondence in *The Times*, especially carried on by Sir John Lubbock himself, his opponent Sir J. Bundell Maple, and Mr J. A. Stacey, the secretary of the Early Closing Association. On 11 May *The Times* contained a protest against the bill signed by leading London West End firms, including Debenham and Freebody, Dickens and Jones, Liberty & Co, Marshall and Snelgrove, Peter Robinson, Swan and Edgar, and the London Chamber of Commerce. The firms concerned made it clear that they sympathised with the object of the bill, that they themselves would be unaffected by it, but that they considered voluntary action to be achieving the end desired without any 'tyrannical and unprecedented interference' with the liberty of the subject which such a bill contemplated. It seems amazing that such businessmen, especially in the light of the accumulated experience of fifty years, could really believe that what they had done was going to be copied by hundreds of small firms, working under very different conditions, if no other pressure than the opinion of people banded in early closing associations was to be applied.

This protest called forth letters from Sir John Lubbock and Mr Stacey. The former pointed out that the majority of those affected by the bill favoured it—it was the selfish minority that necessitated it. Most of the large cities had had meetings supporting the bill; the trade councils of London, Liverpool and Manchester favoured it; more than fifty tradesmen's associations in the country supported it. Mr Stacey was more pungent, declaring that one of the firms which signed the protest was being strongly criticised for lengthening its hours. He denied that hours were being effectively shortened, making the significant statement: 'We are not everywhere holding our own.' For the first time a note of party controversy entered the struggle, for Mr Stacey went on: 'While the various provincial trade associations have shown that Sir John Lubbock's Bill can be safely passed in their own interests and without inconveniencing customers, a small section of London traders has led some of the London Conservative members to go against it. The latter will regret it if they make this a party question.' He thought that some had already suspected that they had put their money on the wrong horse in following Sir Blundell Maple. He continued:

Conservative members should all remember the great and lasting credit achieved by their party in factory legislation. Early Closing legislation is but the corollary and natural supplement of work which largely created the Conservative working man and which, if passed by the Government, will undoubtedly strengthen it among our myriad shopkeepers and shopworkers. It should not be forgotten that the late Samuel Morley and other men who had excellent means of judging the wants of shopkeepers urged the Early Closing Association twenty years ago to adopt a legislative programme.

In a reply next day Sir J. Blundell Maple evaded the main points by claiming that the Shop Hours' Regulation Act—mainly ineffective as we have seen—and voluntary efforts had met the situation; he affected amusement that Mr Stacey, an advanced radical and member of the National Liberal Club, should try to intimidate the Conservatives, and asserted: 'He is wrong in inferring that the Factory Acts limit the hours of adult male labour; but no doubt he would rejoice and laugh in his sleeve if such Radical planks as the thin end of local option and interference with the liberty of the subject could be legalised through the Shops (Early Closing) Bill.' He quoted in support of his position a leading article in *The Times* on the second reading of the bill, which said: 'If it be carried it will subject the liberty to work of adult males to the judgement or the wishes of their neighbours. This is hardly consistent with our British idea of individual freedom.'

Later correspondence led to a challenge from Mr Stacey to Sir J. Blundell Maple to give a single instance of the Voluntary Early Closing Association achieving an improvement in hours which endured for three months—an important point as we have seen. There is no record that Sir Blundell met the challenge!

There is a modern note in a letter of Sir John Lubbock, on 4 September, in which he explained that as the government would not grant time for his bill the serious opposition of a handful of members could block it, even though it passed the Grand Committee on Trade. In his time he had secured the passage of some twenty-five bills but they were generally taken in the small hours of the morning, whereas now 'all opposed business is stopped at midnight and the Government are gradually taking more and more of the time of the House'.

In a letter six days later Sir John summarised the support his bill had had in recent months and years. He said petitions from London tradesmen in favour of the bill numbered 12,000 signatures with hardly any against. The bill received the unanimous support of a House of Commons committee in 1888 and a resolution of the House in 1893 was passed unanimously. It passed a second reading without a division in 1895 and 1896. It passed a Select Committee of the House in 1895 and the Grand Committee on Trade in 1896. Town meetings in large cities had voted in favour of the bill; not one had carried a vote against the bill. Nearly a hundred tradesmen's associations had expressed support for the bill and only one or two had opposed it.

A letter from Mr Frank Debenham, written from Eastbourne, claimed that success had been achieved there by the Voluntary Early Closing Association and stated that similar success had been attained by similar means in Worthing. This called forth a strong denial, as far as Worthing was concerned, from Mr G. E. Smith, the chairman of the committee of the Worthing branch of the Voluntary Early Closing Association. He said, 'I have never been associated with any effort which has so unmistakably failed.' He had been in business for over thirty years in Worthing and he could not recollect any winter before the last, when the campaign for early closing was carried on, 'when there has been so much friction, unpleasantness, and irregularity with regard to closing'. Consequently the members of his committee, he believed without exception, had 'come to the conclusion that Sir John Lubbock's Bill, or one on similar lines, is necessary'.

Mr Stacey dealt with the claim for Eastbourne by saying that the Early Closing Association had been in touch with the town for twenty years and had seen success and failure follow each other through the period. The closing now at 2pm on Wednesday concerned only the drapers, bootmakers and tailors—all the other shops refused to close because of the opposition of a few: some

of those closed at 5pm on Wednesdays but the others at 8pm.
He added that at Hastings a well-organised effort had failed to
win a half-holiday. The result of a canvas had shown the clothiers
and hatters in favour by 29-3; the drapers by 45-19; the furnishing houses by 16-5; and the ironmongers and oilmen by 25-3.
Obviously nothing but compulsion could bring uniformity there.

In April Mr H. E. V. Duncombe, supported by Colonel
Dalbrae, Mr T. Richardson, Mr H. S. Samuel and Mr E. Flower,
introduced a bill to enforce a closing of shops not later than 2pm
on one day a week.[31] This fared no better than Sir John Lubbock's efforts and it is difficult to understand why it was introduced. Then followed a bill on more comprehensive lines, which
was introduced by Sir Charles Dilke on behalf of the National
Union of Shop-Assistants.[32] By this all shops—except chemists'
shops, refreshment houses, tobacco shops, newspaper shops and
book stalls at a railway station, fruit shops and public houses—
would be compelled to close on one day a week at or before 1pm,
on three days a week at or before 7pm, on one day a week at or
before 9pm, and on one day at or before 10pm. It provided that
'all shops shall be kept closed on Sunday throughout the day',
and imposed a penalty of £5 for non-observance of this regulation and the other time regulations. This in itself would have
secured the closing of shops on Sunday, which the old, inadequate penalty under the act of 1677 had long failed, in many
places, to achieve. That such a clause appeared in this bill shows
how anxious the shop-assistants were to put an end to the unnecessary opening of shops on Sunday. By the bill nobody was to
be employed in or about a shop more than half an hour after the
official closing of the shop—except on twenty days in the year,
when a person could be employed up to three hours extra a day,
providing an inspector had been notified during the December
of the previous year.

The duty of enforcing all the regulations of the bill was placed
on inspectors appointed under the Factory and Workshops' Act.
The bill not only provided for the fixing of hours—the day for

early closing and other details of the bill were to be decided by county or borough councils—but for the other reforms that experience had shown were needed. The inclusion of these demands in the bill illustrates the conditions under which many assistants lived and worked. For example, every shop was to provide sitting accommodation for female employees and they must be allowed to use it when not engaged in other duties. No young person or woman must be employed continuously for more than five hours without an interval of at least half an hour for a meal. In any case all employees must be allowed at least an hour for dinner between noon and 2pm and at least half an hour for tea between 4pm and 7pm. Shops and sleeping accommodation for assistants 'shall be kept in a cleanly state and free from all effluvia arising from any drain, privy, or other nuisance, and shall be ventilated in an efficient and suitable manner'. Proper sanitary conveniences were to be provided for all shops, and separate accommodation where persons of both sexes were employed.

The bill, supported by Mr John Burns (later to be the first working-man cabinet minister) among others, did not get a second reading but its publication marked quite clearly the aims of the assistants themselves, indicating that they felt that a bolder challenge was needed than that presented for so long by Sir John Lubbock on behalf of the Early Closing Association; and it brought to the front a new champion of the interests of the shopworkers in Sir Charles Dilke. Trade journals such as the *Drapers' Record*, the *Grocer*, the *Grocers' Journal* and *Drapery World* condemned the bill but the *Shop-Assistant* claimed it was workable because in Cardiff and other large towns the hours worked by many shops were identical with those stipulated in the bill. This illustrates again the fact that the heart of the difficulty about long hours was in the mass of smallish shops which, for various reasons, did not follow the lead of big businesses dealing with customers of the wealthy classes.

This fact was summed up in an article in a monthly review, *Tomorrow*, written by Mr A. Cameron Corbett, MP.[33] In the

July number for 1896 he wrote: 'In the richer parts of our towns there is, undoubtedly, an immense improvement. Changes in the habits of the wealthier classes have made late shopping inconvenient and public opinion has maintained the half-holiday. When you get away, however, from such influences there has been no appreciable progress, and the latest neighbourhoods are today as late as they were in years gone by.' The same writer has this comment on the act limiting the hours of young people: 'Much good has been done by the convictions that have been secured, and the admonitions that have been given, but the great majority of the sufferers must remain unrelieved until we secure legislation that will be easily enforced, that will be enforced without requiring them to face the terrible danger of giving evidence against their employers.'

The Shop-Assistants' Union backed the re-introduction of Sir Charles Dilke's bill in 1898 but this was again unsuccessful. However, one feature of it was soon secured. By an act of 9 August 1899 it was stated that in all retail shops where women assistants worked, seats must be provided behind the counter for their use in the proportion of not less than one seat for every three women employed in that room.[34] This was not secured without opposition but as it only applied to women it did not meet with the full attack of those who shuddered at any legislation which interfered with men's hours or conditions.

The efforts to secure this act had been supported by a special section of the Early Closing Association which was formed for the purpose under the name of 'The League to Secure Seats for Women in Shops'. At a meeting called by this body and attended by representatives of the drapery and other trades, Mr Frank Debenham and others opposed the proposed legislation but some employers from the London suburbs supported it. Mr Debenham had already set out his arguments in a long letter to *The Times*. He said that most West End houses had provided seats and given opportunity for short rests in the day and, although he admitted that this was not universal, he claimed that the conditions for women 'have been ameliorated to a remarkable extent' and that 'even among traders whose business lies among the working classes where competition in business, custom, habits, and, frequently, the necessities of the working classes themselves prevent the full extension of these improved conditions to the assistants, some progress has been made and is still going on'.[35]

The competition between the Early Closing Association and the Voluntary Early Closing Association continued,[36] with the latter claiming great improvement in hours secured yearly and Sir John Lubbock, on behalf of the former, stating in December 1898 that 'On the whole I believe that the hours are now longer than ever'. Sir John said this at a meeting for women called by the Early Closing Association in London. Mrs Creighton, the wife of the Bishop of London (who presided), said: 'Legislation would certainly be necessary to attain the object of the association, and, if that legislation was to be secured, it would be necessary for the assistants to show, with more spirit and energy than they had yet displayed, that they were ready to help themselves, and for the public generally to support the labours of the association.'[37] But the assistants continued, in general, apathetic. Many feared the loss of employment if they showed an interest in even the Early Closing Association and few had the time or energy after their working day to support it. Those with spirit and energy had, in many cases, the ambition to set up their own business one day and they were not sure that they wanted any restriction upon their freedom to work, and to make others work, whatever hours seemed likely to mean success when that day came.[38]

In 1899 the Early Closing Association organised a national testimonial to Sir John Lubbock and asked each assistant to subscribe three pence. In all 10,000 subscribers, all assistants, provided a pair of silver vases which were presented to Sir John, who had become Lord Avebury, at the annual meeting of the association in March 1900.[39] In acknowledging the gift Lord Avebury said that 'While other classes of workers were agitating for an

J

eight-hour day, shopmen, and still worse, shopwomen, were working in many places as much as fourteen hours a day'.

The difficulty of organising the pressure of public opinion to secure its objects was found by the Early Closing Association in a court case in which it was the defendant in the summer of 1899.[40] A draper in the Seven Sisters Road, London, sued the association for attempting to stop people shopping at his business. He claimed that the association had been trying to get a 2pm closing on Thursdays in his area. Most of the drapers did close at 2pm but he could not afford to do so because if he did his customers went to a nearby road where shops were open until 6pm. He said that he closed at 5pm on Thursdays and gave his employees a whole holiday once a month and a fortnight's holiday in the summer. His shop had been picketed by the association with people who distributed handbills which read:

> Is this fair? All the drapers of Seven Sisters Road (with one exception) now close at 1 or 2 o'clock on Thursdays, thus giving much rest to the hardworked assistants. The exception referred to is Messrs Harvard Brothers who refuse the concession granted by their fellow-traders. You are invited to assist the ECA in winning a real half-holiday for shop-assistants. Please shop before 1 on Thursdays and support the early closing firms.

After complaint by the plaintiff the bill had been altered but new ones had been substituted and people posted outside his shop had carried bills asking people to inquire which shops closed at 2pm on Thursday and only to shop there, and saying that overwork in shops caused blighted health. In the courts the association claimed that every word in all the handbills was true but the judge, Mr Justice Wills, in his summing up told the special jury that although the statements were true they must consider whether they applied to the plaintiff in such a way as to be libellous. The jury gave a verdict for the plaintiff of £150 and costs.

The number who tried to evade the Shop Hours' Act and employed young people for excessively long hours is shown by the returns of the London County Council inspectors for 1899. In the 24,035 premises where young people were employed it was found that in 1,635 cases the hours for young people were 80 or under, but in excess of the permitted number, and in 557 over 80 a week. Most of these cases had resulted in a warning to the owner but 87 owners had been prosecuted and 79 of these convicted.[41]

Thus the century closed with the situation in many places no better, and possibly worse, than at the mid-century. Improvements there had been in high-class shops and in certain parts of the country, but these improvements were precarious and very much depended on the whim of an individual who might wreck schemes for shorter hours by refusing to abide by the majority decision.

CHAPTER EIGHT

THE STRUGGLE TO OBTAIN THE
ACT OF 1911

Sir John Lubbock, now as Lord Avebury a member of the House of Lords, continued his campaign for his bill in the Upper House. What follows might be thought farcical were it not tragic. The House of Lords decided to set up a select committee to study the whole subject![1]

The suggestion came in 1900 from the Prime Minister, the Marquis of Salisbury, who said that the subject had not yet been thoroughly considered, at any rate by the peers. This, after the reports of four select committees, was only delaying action on the part of an opponent of legislation on this subject who feared that pressure of growing opinion might force the government to do something. When, following this suggestion, Lord Avebury moved that a select committee be set up in February 1901 Lord Salisbury agreed but pointed out that Lord Avebury's bill was quite different from factory legislation in that it proposed 'that the local authorities, which differ very much in different places, should have the power of determining whether or not men might work during the latter part of the day, and, what is more important, whether consumers of the necessities of life should be allowed to buy them late in the day or not. It is a very striking interference with the liberty both of the consumer and of the shopkeeper.' There was the usual claim of the opponent of shop legislation to be anxious to safeguard the 'ordinary working man' when he added that he hoped that the committee would discover not only what 'merely philanthropic persons with extremely amiable sentiments' thought, but 'what the ordinary working men, who exist in millions, think of the limitation of this power of providing the necessaries of life for themselves and their families . . . and whether they are of opinion that the relief given to the shopmen is adequate to the inconvenience and trouble that they would sustain'. In any case Lord Salibury made it clear that neither the present government nor any other would be bound by any findings of the committee.

A recent writer said of the Marquis of Salisbury that 'reverence for experts struck him as folly',[2] and this no doubt accounts for his contemptuous dismissal of the knowledge of his fellow peer, Lord Avebury, who had behind him a distinguished career as a banker, man of science and author, treasurer of the Royal Society, past president of the London Chamber of Commerce and of the British Association, past chairman of the London County Council and vice-chancellor of the University of London for six years. That a man of such wide interests and expert knowledge had felt it worth while to devote so much of his energy for so many years to the cause of the ignored shopworkers is in itself a proof of the deserts of their case.

His persistence in pressing for legislation in both Houses of Parliament, and his advocacy of the cause outside Parliament, did a very great deal to prepare for the measure of success which was to be achieved before his death in 1913, although, unfortunately, by then memory of his efforts had faded.

The committee, over which Lord Avebury presided and which included Lord Salisbury, presented its report in August 1901.[3] It fully confirmed the claims which Lord Avebury and others

had made for some time that the situation in many shops with
regard to length of hours was as bad as it had been a quarter of
a century before. The hours of shops in many parts of the
country, which are revealed in the evidence given to the committee, have been tabulated in Appendix 2. In addition it will
be worth while to note some statements from the committee's
report or from the evidence which was submitted.

The committee found 'that the subject is one of urgent importance, and that the existing evils show no general or sufficient
sign of amendment. In many places the hours during which
shops are open range as high as eighty to ninety per week, in
addition to which some time is occupied in clearing up, putting
away the goods, and packing up the articles purchased.' It
reported that over 290 tradesmen's associations had shown by
evidence, petition or resolution that they favoured an early
closing bill—many wanted a more stringent one. The only
tradesmen's associations to oppose the bill were the Off-Licence
Holders and the London Pawnbrokers. It had been difficult to
get evidence of the opinion of the poorer classes of the population but the co-operative societies, even if catering for the very
poor, invariably closed early. The representatives of the trade
unions, too, said that early closing would not inconvenience the
workers. Many witnesses had expressed a strong desire that
heavier fines should be provided by legislation for Sunday trading. Finally the committee reported that

> The evidence has convinced us that earlier closing would be an
> immense boon to the shopkeeping community, to shopkeepers
> and shop-assistants alike, that the present hours are grievously
> injurious to health, especially in the case of women, and under
> these circumstances we recommend that town councils should be
> authorised to pass Provisional Orders, making such regulations in
> respect to the closing of shops as may seem to them to be neces-
> sary for the areas under their jurisdiction; and these Provisional
> Orders should be submitted to Parliament in the usual manner
> before acquiring the force of law.

Miss Octavia Hill in her evidence to the committee claimed, on the basis of conversations with people in Stepney, Limehouse, Southwark, Westminster, Marylebone, Lisson Grove and the High Street, Notting Hill, that consumers wanted an earlier closing because the men would then have to bring their wages home earlier and would not have the opportunity to spend the money in the public houses before their wives got it. Mr George Snape, of the Wolverhampton Grocers' Association, said that wages were paid on Friday night or by 1pm on Saturday so that there was no need for late shopping on Friday or Saturday there. Yet he showed that grocers' shops were open until 9pm on Friday and 11pm on Saturday. He pointed out, too, that hours were longer in his town now than they had been thirty years before. Then the leading grocers had closed at 7pm on the first four nights of the week; this had continued for half a dozen years and then newcomers had remained open longer and the closing hours were now 8pm on the first three nights of the week. The shops did not close at 2pm on Thursday. Mr J. B. Redfern of the Bradford Grocers' Association supported the view that working hours had increased, claiming that this had been the tendency in Bradford for the last ten years.

Mr C. L. Abraham, representing the National Chamber of Trade of Hull and District, said, 'I have never in the whole course of my experience heard objections from the general public to the earlier closing of shops. On the other hand I have always thought they were either indifferent to the matter or would prefer to have earlier closing.' From Plymouth came the opinion of a member of the co-operative society, with its experience of earlier closing, in the person of Mr Henry Evans who suggested that 'shopping is a matter of education. You can educate your customers to come at any time you like. If you kept open an hour later, I suggest that you would do the same trade; if you closed an hour earlier, I suggest you would do nothing less.' This, of course, would only operate where there was a uniform closing hour. The point of importance is that those who argued that the wishes and needs of the consumer necessitated late hours had really no case.

The secretary of the Early Closing Association, Mr J. A. Stacey, speaking from an experience of twenty years, said that he thought that in many districts of London people liked the shops to be open late as the lights made the streets gay and the streets were the only places for people to promenade and find recreation. He was not, of course, advocating late hours but stating a fact which revealed a social problem. The evils of that way of meeting the problem outweighed any merit it might have, for not only was the health of shopworkers—employers and employees—being sacrificed but, in many cases, the practice of late shopping had its victims among the shoppers too.

At least that was the opinion of the Rev F. J. W. Horsley, rector of St Peter's, Walworth, who told the committee, 'I do not think the effect of this late shopping upon infant mortality has been sufficiently considered. Roughly speaking, a quarter of our babies die before they are a year old, and I believe it is very largely due to their being kept out so late at night, and being taken into public houses with all their accompanying smell and heat. A large number of the babies are shopping till midnight.' It might be argued that to shut the shops would not prevent the mothers visiting and staying at the public houses; indeed, it might drive more of them there. But it seems safe to conclude that in many cases, deprived of the excuse to go out to look at the shops and make late purchases, the mothers would remain at home.

An argument that reads strangely today was advanced by Miss Nora Vynne who represented the Freedom of Labour Defence Association. She considered that shops must be free to remain open as long as they wished, or there would be no competition between them and prices would rise. She saw good, not evil, resulting from shops staying open late but she did admit the hours of assistants should be shortened.

Sir John Blundell Maple, still president of the Voluntary Early

Closing Association, argued that the success achieved by the voluntary method obviated the need for legislation, and the proceedings were enlivened by a duel of words between him and the chairman of the committee. From this it became clear that the Voluntary Association was really run by the owners of some of the large London stores—Mr Marshall of Marshall & Snelgrove was the treasurer, Mr Debenham of Debenham & Freebody the chairman of the committee—and that its chief objective now was to obtain increased facilities for cheap half-day excursions to the seaside—Brighton for 2s 6d return being quoted as an example.

It is significant that Lord Avebury, from the chair, stated at one day's sitting of the committee that apart from the witnesses that day against the bill no others representing tradesmen's associations had applied to be heard in opposition to it. Of those associations opposing legislation one was the National Federation of Off-Licensees, represented by Mr John Parker, who said that the federation thought 'that domestic shops of all kinds should not be subject to interference by law as to the hours of opening and closing, and that any evils connected with the employment of assistants for long hours should be dealt with in an exclusive measure'. Mr Charles Thompson, representing the National Pawnbrokers' Association, proved to be a most unreliable witness whose attempts to bluff the committee that he knew more than he did of the general situation broke down under cross-examination. Similarly Mr Henry Davison, representing the Metropolitan Pawnbrokers' Protection Society, made general statements about the inconvenience which the bill would cause to small shopkeepers, but when asked to give specific instances was at a loss to provide any. In any case he claimed that any man could work without injury to health for sixty-five to seventy hours a week.

Mr Abraham of Hull, whose evidence was referred to above, mentioned a national conference of tradesmen's associations which had met in London in June 1900. It had been presided over by Sir James Woodhouse, MP, and Sir Charles Dilke, MP, and Mr Lloyd George, MP, had been present. Those represented at the meeting included tradesmen's associations at Blackpool, Bolton, Bournemouth, Burnley, Chatham, Dewsbury, Halifax, Huddersfield, Hull, Morley, Newark, North Staffordshire, Ossett, Plymouth & Stonehouse, Glamorganshire, Merthyr Tydfil, Somercotes Riddings, Southport, Tunbridge Wells, Wakefield, West Yorkshire; and the London Master Bakers' Association, National Pawnbrokers' Association, Metropolitan Grocers' Association, and Drapers' Chamber of Trade. The conference wanted legislation to shorten hours and passed a resolution stating 'That any bill for the regulation of shop hours should fix the maximum number of hours per week that shops may be kept open, and this conference recommends that such maximum hours be sixty-eight, including meal times, and that the basis of the closing hours be fixed at three days in the week at 8.30pm, one day at 1pm, one day at 9pm and one day at 11pm'. It was emphasised that these were the maximum hours and that shorter hours than these already prevailed in some places.

One witness, Mr John Williams, president of the Manchester, Salford & District Grocers' Association, said that small shopkeepers with no assistants desired legislation enforcing shorter hours because they were too suspicious of each other to close voluntarily. One of them told him, 'About 9 o'clock I go to the door to see if they are closing at the other corner. If they are not shaping to close I wait until half-past nine, then I put up the shutters, but do not close the door, then the other party puts up his shutters, and we wait for each other perhaps up to 11 o'clock, or until one of us gets tired and we close and go to bed, too tired to care whether the other fellow is closed or not.'

Evidence of the working of the Shop Hours' Act of 1892 in London was given by Mr Alfred Spencer, the chief officer of the Public Control Department of the London County Council. He said that in 1899 and 1900 many young people were working 80, 90 or even 100 hours a week although the act only allowed 74 hours. However, as a result of warnings, advice and 285 prosecutions he felt the position now warranted his saying that 'the Shop Hours' Acts are now in London fairly and almost strictly observed'. He considered that in consequence of the acts the number of boys between the ages of fourteen and eighteen employed by shops had been reduced and an increased use had been made of schoolchildren who were employed for an hour or two before school time and several hours in the evening. He believed that seventy-four hours was too long a working week for young people and he felt that there was a need to limit the hours of adult women.

In spite of the findings of the committee and the weight of evidence supporting the need for legislation nothing was done by Parliament in 1901. Earlier in the year Sir Charles Dilke had introduced the bill,[4] which he had sponsored before, fixing definite closing hours for shops and limiting the total hours of employment for all assistants to sixty a week. His supporters included Mr John Burns and Mr Lloyd George. But it did not reach a second reading. Unfortunately the supporters of Avebury and Dilke played into the hands of those opposed to any legislation by attacking each other. Mr Stacey, of the Early Closing Association, said that Avebury's bill 'did not ask for all they would like but it asked for all they are likely to get within the next or many generations'.[5] The National Union of Shop-Assistants described the bill as unworkable.[6] Speakers of the Traders' Defence League said that to try to close shops by law 'is undesirable and impracticable', and that 'any restriction on adult labour was un-English and unnecessary'.[7]

Early in 1902 Lord Avebury reintroduced his bill in the House of Lords.[8] It was opposed by Lord Belper, supported by the Bishop of Winchester. The comment of the writer in the *Annual Register* was, 'Its rejection by 57 to 26 votes, with no alternative offered, reflected very little credit on either the government or the majority of the peers'. If the government had not changed its opinion the *Annual Register* had, for only two years before it had approved the rejection of the same bill, describing those who voted against it on that occasion as 'upholders of individual liberty'.

In March 1903 Mr Robert John Price, member for Norfolk East, moved in the House of Commons

> That in the opinion of this House the unnecessarily long hours of labour in shops are injurious to the health and well-being of all concerned; that it is desirable that borough and district councils should be authorised to obtain provisional orders making such regulations in respect to the closing of shops and the limitations of hours of labour of shopworkers as may seem to them to be necessary for the areas under their jurisdiction, thus effectively carrying out the recommendations of the Select Committee of the House of Lords on the Early Closing of Shops, as embodied in paragraph 15 of the Report of 1901.[9]

Sir John Gorst, member for Cambridge University, in seconding the motion reminded the House that in the 1895 General Election the Conservatives had 'vied with each other in assuring the electors that they would make the social conditions of the people their one consideration. They had no United Kingdom to dismember, and no parliamentary reform to occupy themselves with. They had, in fact, they said, nothing to do but to attend to the social condition of the people. They were returned to power, and practically nothing was done.' He therefore appealed to the government to give practical effect to the findings of the committee of 1901. Mr H. H. Asquith, in supporting the motion, emphasised and broadened the same point, saying, 'It is really a melancholy and discreditable thing that for eighteen years, while both parties in the state had been practically agreed on these two propositions [the evil of long hours and the need for legislative action] nothing really effective had been done, except that very homeopathic measure for shortening the hours of young persons in shops, which does very little, and is, I am afraid, but inadequately administered'.

The die-hard individualist, Sir Frederick Banbury, brought

up the rather thread-bare case of the poor shopkeeper, ready to keep open to earn a little more, and said, 'What is wanted is not so much legislation as the freedom of every man to manage his own affairs in the way he thought best for his own interest.' He voiced the reason why many who lacked his stubborn laissez-faire doctrines hesitated over the only legislation that would be effective, when he said, 'Up to the present there has been no legislation affecting the hours of labour of the adult male'.

Mr John Burns added his support to the motion, pointing out that, 'Mechanics now had short hours but they were inclined to rather selfishly impose long hours on the people who served them. The shopkeeper's assistant ought to get protection from the too often selfish and greedy mechanic, whose wife too frequently bought the Sunday dinner at midnight on Saturday night.' Here, of course, the speaker put his finger on one of the reasons why it was so difficult to get the smaller shops to close early. Their customers who worked, or whose husbands worked, much shorter hours than shop-assistants were not prepared to alter their own habits to enable another class of worker to enjoy similar conditions to their own. It was not, as a rule, the wealthy section of the community which demanded long hours for shops and, as forthright Mr Burns put it, 'If Belgravia could shop at the Army and Navy Stores between ten and five o'clock, I see no reason why something like reasonable hours should not be kept in the New Cut'.

In spite of what had been said, implying that the government was really pledged to legislate, the Home Secretary, Mr A. Akers-Douglas, told the House that there was too much legislation under consideration for the government to introduce a new measure. So, although the House agreed without a division to the motion, nothing was done.

At the same time Lord Avebury had reintroduced his bill into the House of Lords.[10] An attempt to anticipate it by another measure on the subject by Lord Ribblesdale[11] was defeated by a ruling of the lord chancellor, and Lord Avebury's bill passed all the stages in the House of Lords and was sent to the House of Commons. There no time was provided for its consideration. Sir Charles Dilke equally met with no success in reintroducing his bill to the House of Commons. The National Union of Shop-Assistants continued to oppose Lord Avebury's bill, condemning it at its annual conference at Manchester and at a great protest meeting in St James's Hall on 18 June.[12] All this must have been very confusing to the public and it played into the hands of the government who obviously intended to postpone any legislation as long as it possibly could.

In February 1904 Sir Charles Dilke once more brought in his bill but it made no progress. Next month deputations from associations—the Early Closing Association, the National Union of Shop-Assistants, and the National Association of Grocers' Assistants—visited the Home Office to urge the government to introduce an early closing bill.[13] Mr Cameron Corbett, MP, as chairman of the Early Closing Association, pressed for a bill on the lines of Lord Avebury's measure, but said that his association could not support Dilke's bill as it was impracticable. The Shop-Assistants contended, in their interview, that legislation must provide for uniform closing and must be enforced by town and county councils. They also claimed that Sunday trading was unnecessary and must be prohibited. The Grocers supported Avebury's bill.

In April the government introduced a bill into the House of Commons which was modelled on Avebury's bill which had passed the Lords in the previous year.[14] The second reading took place on 1 June when the bill passed by 130 to 42. Early in the debate Sir Charles Dilke stated that he would divide the House against the bill on the grounds that it was 'unduly hampered by restrictions and, not providing for the regulation of the hours of shop-assistants, fails to satisfy the terms of the unanimous Resolution of the House'. He reminded the House that to close a shop at a certain hour was no guarantee that the assistants would cease work then or even soon after that hour.

It was chiefly those who thought, like Sir Charles, that the bill would be of little value, who recorded votes against it. There was, of course, the opposition of Sir Frederick Banbury, who made the usual statements about the hardships of the small shop-keepers and the unnecessary interference with the liberty of the individual. He contended that he 'must confess that the principle of the bill was one which he should never have thought would have been brought forward by a Conservative Government'. Mr Asquith, for the Opposition, supported the bill although regarding it as a very mild measure of reform. Significantly he added that he had given a great deal of attention to this subject for many years, and he was satisfied that no measure would be really effective which did not couple with the power of compulsorily closing the shop itself some sanction by which the shop-assistants should not be employed unless for a short interval after the closing hour. If any of the people who wanted more drastic reform thought from Mr Asquith's statement that the next Liberal Government would move swiftly in the matter they were to be disappointed.

The act of 1904[15] provided that a local authority might make an order, which had to be confirmed by the central authority, fixing a closing hour for shops not earlier than 7pm except on one day when it could not be earlier than 1pm. The order could define the shops or trades to which it applied. An order would not apply to post offices, chemists, places selling intoxicating liquors or tobacco, refreshment rooms or newspaper shops. The act was permissive and no authority was compelled to apply it but, if it proposed to do so, it must give notice of its intention, receive and consider objections and only make the order if at least two-thirds of the occupiers of the shops concerned approved. Even then the central authority might disallow the order. If an order was in force it could be annulled if the local authority were satisfied that the occupants of the majority of shops concerned were opposed to a continuance of the order.

That the act achieved little is claimed in a paragraph in the annual report of the National Union of Shop-Assistants, published in 1905, which reads:

> The year 1904 has seen the passing of the Shop Hours' Act. The union may congratulate itself upon its foresight and upon its policy in respect of this Gilbertian piece of legislation. It is a rather curious fact, that when we opposed the measure as a bill, on account of its rather unworkable nature, we were roundly abused by its supporters. Now it has become an act its principal promoters are testifying to the soundness of our objections, and are already getting weary of trying to make it operative.

Mr J. A. Stacey, secretary of the Early Closing Association, writing to the press on 20 January 1905, says,

> In September, the Board of Management [of the Early Closing Association] were hard at work canvassing the most favourable areas for the statutory two-thirds majority of traders. Unfortunately, they have not succeeded at a single point. While it seems to be clear that these cannot be obtained in the poorer parts of London, Glasgow, Liverpool, Manchester, and other great cities, it appears to be equally certain that the local authorities, even if they would, cannot put the act into operation without them.[16]

Lord Avebury was not prepared to take as gloomy a view of the prospects as Mr Stacey and he claimed that the act enabled a majority of tradesmen to settle the hours of closing, 'and this is what the Early Closing Association has so long contended for'.[17] It seems, however, that the act secured very little, if any, improvement.

The comparative failure of the act was generally admitted in a debate in the House of Commons on 1 May 1907.[18] Mr Shackleton, who represented Clitheroe, moved, 'That in the opinion of this House, more drastic legislation with regard to the closing of shops and the hours of shop-assistants is required'. He said that the number of orders made under the act of 1904 was very few because local authorities were not bound to act, even if the necessary two-thirds of the shopkeepers asked them to do so. He instanced the fact that recently at Dover twenty-four out of twenty-eight hairdressers applied for an order but were refused because the council said that a *prima facie* case had not been made out.

Speaking later in the debate the home secretary in the Liberal Government, which followed the general election of 1906, Mr H. J. Gladstone, agreed that in England and Wales only 112 orders, affecting 9,000 shops and perhaps 15,000 people, out of probably 800,000 assistants, had been made. Of these orders ninety-two affected one trade only. In districts where the restrictions of the act were most needed, as for example in London and Manchester, nothing had been done. He continued: 'The difficulties which the act has produced are enough to make weak-hearted people avoid it. It is difficult to obtain a two-thirds majority for this or any other purpose. An undue protection of interests has been given by law to the exclusion of the rights which the act was designed to protect.' On the other hand Mr Gladstone was very cautious, not to say discouraging, on the prospects of new legislation. Dilke's bill—which he regularly brought forward— would take a long time to pass and the Home Office already had a list of twenty bills which it would take two years to pass. He did not attempt to explain why this subject was so unimportant that, after all the lip-service paid to it, any bill to implement resolutions of Parliament must wait its turn until the House had disposed of some twenty other matters. The Liberal Government was certainly fully occupied in laying—without knowing it—the foundations of the Welfare State. But that the care of shop-assistants ought to be high on its list of priorities did not occur to it.

Mr Seddon of Lancashire, who had been a shop-assistant, speaking in the debate pointed out that where orders under the 1904 act had been obtained they were often in places that already had shorter hours than normal. He claimed that thirty-five per cent of shop-assistants fell victims to chest complaints and that nearly fifty per cent of the patients in one well-known sanatorium were girls who had been shop-assistants. He, and the

K

member for Fulham, Mr T. Davies, pressed for a sixty-hour week.

Characteristically, Sir F. Banbury claimed that the act was a failure because it was not required and he voiced openly what it seems, at least in part, the Liberal Government and many people, inside and outside Parliament, still felt, but were ashamed to say. He maintained that the adult male should be free to use his labour as he saw fit. If he chose to work twenty hours a day he should be allowed to do so, and was to be respected for his physical capacity.

The position outlined by the home secretary did not improve much in the coming months for in 1909 the government published a return of the closing orders, made under the act of 1904, covering the period from the first operation of the act to 31 December 1908.[19] In that period only 9 county councils (in four of these only one small area was affected and in only one more than ten areas), 91 borough councils and 72 urban district councils had made orders in England and Wales. These affected 14,080 shops.

In 1905 and 1906 those interested in securing better conditions for the shopworkers were once again concerned about the number of shops which opened on Sundays.[20] Lord Avebury was responsible, in March 1906, for a motion which produced what the *Annual Register* called 'a noteworthy debate', calling on the government to give serious attention to the matter. In the following January a message to the nation from the primate, the Roman Catholic Archbishop of Westminster, and the president of the National Council of Evangelical Free Churches called for a 'better observance of Sunday' and in March 1907 Lord Avebury once more pressed, in the House of Lords, for legislation to control the Sunday opening of shops. Earl Beauchamp made one of the stock answers of a government that wishes to avoid touching a difficult subject. He said, on behalf of the government, that their hands were full and the subject one of great difficulty in detail.

In 1909 a bill to close all shops on Sunday, except those engaged in the liquor trade, refreshment places, shops selling newspapers, milk and cream, and chemist shops, was before the House of Commons.[21] Certain other shops, such as those selling bread, could open until 9am. Except that the penalties for opening shops illegally were increased it does not seem that the bill made any great change in the Sunday Observance Act of 1677, and as a private bill, introduced by Sir John Kennaway, it did not get far in the House. By August a government bill proposed to deal with the matter.

The Shopkeepers' and Small Traders' Protection Association which fought to prevent legislation interfering with the freedom of the shopkeeper to open for whatever hours he liked on any day of the week, including Sunday (although Sunday opening was illegal), started a monthly paper, called the *Shopkeeper*, in September 1908.[22] It lasted only until June 1909 so it evidently did not win much support, which would seem to indicate that the association itself was hardly popular with those whom it claimed to represent. In the first issue the reason for the paper, a four page production, is stated to be 'the necessity for some medium through which the small trader and shopkeeper may be informed of various attempts made from time to time to interfere with him', because 'on all sides the small trader is being attacked'. Its readers are warned, 'Don't forget, a bill such as Sir Charles Dilke's Shops Bill would ruin you'. In the November number the editor urged his readers to combine against 'those Associations and Big Traders who are working for early weekday and Sunday closing'.

The pressure for legislation in the country was, however, now so strong that the paper evidently felt that some measure would become law and it therefore put forward its own suggestions. They were that the assistants should be protected in the following ways and the owners left free to open when he liked. The proposals were that no employee, except members of the owner's family, should work more than a fixed number of hours a week—

no actual number is suggested; and every employee should have one day's rest in seven with a safeguard that no employee should be penalised for refusing to work on Sunday on conscientious grounds.

Reference was made to local associations at Leicester, Kilburn and Worcester. The latter, 200 strong, was formed when, in 1905, an attempt, which failed, was made to put the 1904 act into operation. The March 1909 number mentioned efforts of the association to prevent attempts made in various places to close shops and markets on Sunday, and carried a strong attack on 'Sabbatarianism' which, it said, was 'again bursting with energy'.

Sir Charles Dilke tried again with his bill, on the lines of the one he had introduced in 1904 and 1905, in February 1909,[23] but that was not proceeded with as the government announced in the King's Speech of the same month that it intended to introduce legislation of a similar nature. This bill was debated in the House of Commons on 4 August 1909.[24] It proposed that shop-assistants should not be employed for more than sixty hours (exclusive of meal times) in any week, and should not work after 8pm on more than three days in a week. Overtime up to thirty days, for not more than two hours a day, was to be allowed.

Every shop was to be closed not later than 2pm on one day a week, but local authorities could suspend this provision in holiday resorts for a period of not more than four months in a year. All shops were to close on Sunday, except in Jewish areas or areas where it had been customary to hold a street market in London, and in such places the shops could be open until 2pm. If two-thirds of the occupiers of affected shops in any area asked the local authority it was allowed to fix a closing hour in the evenings not earlier than 7pm and substitute 1pm for 2pm as the closing time on the half-holiday. Provision was to be made for one seat for every three women employees; proper ventilation and suitable and sufficient sanitary conveniences were to be installed. Shops doing post office business were exempt from the bill, which was not to apply to a rural parish of less than one thousand inhabitants, unless the county council approached the home secretary on the matter. The time allowed for meals was based on the length of employment in the day—half an hour if working six hours but less than eight; three-quarters of an hour if working eight but less than ten; one hour if working ten but less than twelve; and one and a half hours if working twelve hours or more.

The following premises were exempt from the weekly half-holiday and Sunday closing provisions : those selling liquor (also exempt from the 8pm closing regulation), refreshments and fruit, tobacco, bread, confectionery, newspapers and periodicals, motor and cycle accessories, cream and milk; and also railway bookstalls and refreshment rooms. The penalties imposed for any breach of the law were £1 for the first offence, £5 for the second, and £20 for the third.

The Home Secretary, Mr H. J. Gladstone, in introducing the bill said, with reference to the clause about Sunday closing: 'The competition in retail business, I regret to say, has led to a constantly increasing tendency to open on Sundays, not because the shopkeepers desire it but because somebody opens, and then the rest must open in order to keep their trade. We have found an almost unanimous feeling among shopkeepers, and, of course, among shop-assistants, in favour of the closing of shops on Sundays.' Mr Gladstone calculated that the bill would affect a million shop-assistants and half a million owners. He admitted that conditions of employment varied very much through the country and that, while some conditions were excellent, 'there are a multitude of others where the conditions are atrocious'. In such cases, he stated, assistants were working eighty and some over ninety hours a week.

Mr Horatio Bottomley was a vociferous opponent of the first reading, classing the bill as an example of the 'parental system of government' which was becoming an obsession of the administration. He said that he had no objection to the limiting of the hours of shop-assistants but queried what Sunday closing had to do with that, stating, 'I thought we had heard the last about that in the present Parliament.' In spite of his opposition the bill was given a first reading, but as the home secretary had stated that it had been introduced to promote discussion it probably surprised few members that it was dropped. On 20 August Mr J. Seddon expressed in the House the regret of the shop-assistants that this was done and the hope that the bill would be taken in the next session.

Mr Seddon had recently been elected as Labour MP for the Newton division of Lancashire, his candidature being supported by the National Union of Shop-Assistants. The union hoped to amend the bill[25] so that the sixty hours of normal work included meal times, and these of adequate duration, and to secure 1pm as the hour of the half-holiday closing. A meeting in Hyde Park was attended by 10,000 people in pouring rain to press for these amendments and other meetings were held in Sheffield, Leeds and South Wales. The union felt that the bill so amended might prove to be 'the base of what might be a Shop-Assistants' Charter'.

The year 1910, with general elections in January and December, the death of Edward VII in May, and the heated controversy over the powers of the House of Lords running all through it, was not a propitious time for a measure of reform so long delayed and so uncertainly championed by the government as the Shops' Bill. Sir Charles Dilke introduced his bill[26] again in February and it was down for a second reading in June but by then the business of the House had been disorganised by the event of the king's death.

Then in July Mr Winston Churchill as home secretary introduced a measure which was really the same bill as that of the previous year.[27] In doing so he remarked that the shop-assistants could not improve conditions themselves, that the shopkeepers had tried and failed to do something by agreement, and that 'both sections ably supported by the public, and energetically supported by a section of the public, have attempted to effect these alterations of hours, and both have succeeded so little that I think we are entitled to say that voluntary effort in this direction has conclusively failed'. He was not very optimistic about finding time to pass the bill in this session if there was serious opposition. The chief opposers at the time were again Sir Frederick Banbury and Mr Horatio Bottomley, and in November the bill was withdrawn without explanation.

While there was still the possibility of the bill getting a second reading Mr Stacey, the secretary of the Early Closing Association, made some revealing comments about the attitude of various sections of the shopkeeping world to it, in a letter to *The Times*.[28] He said that some proprietors who closed early felt that the bill did not go far enough to bring the others into line while others denounced the bill as unnecessary government interference. Employees differed in their attitude in proportion to the treatment they received from their employers. Very few showed any altruism. Many were the sons and daughters of farmers, professional men and shopkeepers who were suspicious of associating themselves with anything that savoured of trade unionism. The Early Closing Association itself, as was to be expected from the fact that its main support had always come from employers, did not like the Labour Party as its ally, for Stacey wrote:

So far as the Labour Party champion the bill their advocacy is to be received with suspicion. The contribution of trade unionism to early closing gains in shops and warehouses so far is practically nil. The average assistant is greatly more in sympathy with his employer in the matter of hours and wages than is the average mechanic. If real sympathy with shopworkers exists, an authoritative outcry on the part of trade unionism against late shopping habits of its members could well be made. In districts where artisans and their families form a large section of shoppers, where sons and husbands cease work early, our appeals to shop early and so help others to win a portion of the leisure they themselves enjoy require the most vigorous continuance.

In a later letter Mr Stacey said that his association supported the bill but did not regard it as a solution to the problem of late closing. A simpler, stricter bill was needed. He claimed

> that the harsher an Early Closing Bill appears to the ordinary
> person the more popular it is with the ordinary shopkeeper. That
> is to say a drastic measure compelling (according to district) a
> 7, 7.30 or 8 o'clock closing ordinarily, a 10 o'clock closing on
> Saturdays, a full half-holiday on one day, and complete closing on
> Sunday, would be far preferable, in the shopkeeping world, to
> anything falling short of it.

The weakening of the bill by the long list of exemptions, for
which Mr Winston Churchill was held responsible, was criticised
in a letter by Mr C. Weller Kent.[29] He stated that

> it was put to me by the representative of a large body of grocers
> and provision merchants that it was unfair to compel grocers in
> provincial towns to close their establishments by 2 o'clock in the
> afternoon on one day each week, while chemists, dairymen,
> bakers, confectioners, refreshment caterers, fruiterers, and other
> traders were allowed to remain open. It is contended by the grocer
> that his usual customer, finding his shop closed, would be driven
> to the chemist, to the dairyman, or to the baker and confectioner
> for the tea, fruit, jam and other commodities generally bought of
> the grocer. Chemists, fruiterers, dairymen and bakers are now
> selling many articles purchasable formerly only from a grocer.

During 1910 the Home Office received deputations from a
number of groups and societies interested in the bill.[30] In July
the representatives of the National Chamber of Trade said they
were in favour of the bill except that they wanted members of a
trader's family to be treated as assistants and not exempted from
the bill's provisions. One speaker, who came from Halifax, said
that under existing legislation it had cost £60 and taken eleven
months to obtain a closing order. Mr Winston Churchill emphasised that he intended to secure a sixty-hour week, exclusive
of meal times, as 'a good, reasonable standard' for assistants. He
repeated this to the deputation from the National Federation of
Meat-Traders in October when that deputation suggested a sixty-
five-hour week for the meat-traders.

In October a deputation from the Federation of Evangelical Free Church Councils in Wales protested that the bill would increase Sunday trading because it repealed the Lord's Day Observance Act of 1677. To this objection the Home Office officials had to admit that in Wales, Sunday trading would be increased, because much of the trading permitted under this bill was illegal by the 1677 act, but that for England the act was in most places a dead letter—Hull was mentioned as an exception. On this subject Mr Churchill said:

> I am in general agreement with you on the great importance— apart altogether from religious considerations on the purely secular question—of making the seventh day a day markedly different in every respect from the other six work-a-day days of the week. I mean that quite apart from any religious argument which may be used, there is immense social importance attaching to that. I should be very sorry indeed if the effect of any legislation for which I was responsible was to promote an approximation between the life which exists among the people on the seventh day and their ordinary daily life.

Similar fear that the bill would cause many shops now closed to open on Sunday was expressed in November by a deputation from the South London Closing of Shops Association. This association had done a lot of work to secure the Sunday closing of shops in south-east London and its work had secured the interest of Lord Avebury and Anglican and Free Church ministers, such as Canon Ottley and Dr Scott Lidgett. To them Mr Churchill suggested that taking the country as a whole the bill would reduce, not extend, Sunday trading. He said: 'Week after week and month after month new shops are opening every Sunday, not only in those little places which cater to the public amusement but even drapers' and ironmongers' shops. It is that very great movement that this clause is designed to counteract. In some parts of the country this clause will have the effect of absolutely arresting any increase of Sunday trading.'

Mr A. O. Goodrich, representing the Metropolitan Association of Grocers, Provision Dealers and Oilmen's Association, said the trade welcomed the clause about Sunday closing. He was leading a deputation on 19 October and he said, with regard to the bill as a whole, that it should be compulsory on all shops to close on the half-holiday. Speaking for his fellow-members of the deputation he said: 'Every gentleman in the room has been engaged in what is called the Voluntary Early Closing Association. We have been engaged in it as masters and men, and unfortunately— I speak for London now—this effort has failed, and failed very largely.'

Two representatives of a deputation of wholesalers championed the cause of the small shopkeeper. One, coming from the North of England, said that seventy-five per cent of the shops had no assistants and that small shopkeepers did not want a half-holiday but did want Sunday closing. A canvas of shopkeepers on the matter of a half-holiday had been made in an area covering about one-fifth of the parliamentary division of Manchester—excluding the city. Of the 4,918 shopkeepers visited, 2,585 had signed a petition against a half-holiday; 852 had refused to sign; and 1,481 had been out when called on and rather guilefully the claim was advanced that all those were opposed to a half-holiday because obviously they were able to take some leisure when it suited them. In the centre of the city 1,200 had signed the petition against a half-holiday.

In reply to a deputation from the Manchester Retail Traders' Association on 28 October, which stated that it did not want a compulsory closing of shops on one half-day a week, Mr Churchill said:

> I am strongly impressed with the opposition there is to what I call the universal half-holiday for shops from the class whom it was designed to benefit, namely, the small shopkeepers. Of course, I have not made up my mind finally, but I am considering whether I will not have to give up that universal half-holiday for shops provision and revert to the provision for a universal half-

holiday to shop-assistants under a heavy penalty and under proper protection.

He went on to point out that a large section of employers did want universal closing and in this he was supported by one of the Home Office officials who was present.

To another deputation, on the same day, from the Drapers' Chamber of Trade, which suggested the compulsory closing of shops at a fixed time each evening, Mr Churchill said, 'I really do not think that the central government is sufficiently supported, and has sufficient driving power to start on this matter of enforcing a universal closing hour all over the country.' He suggested that the case might be met by sending an official to a particular town who should, after consulting the interests concerned, frame a draft order for closing times for the area, which order should come into operation unless one-third of the traders of the town petitioned against it. One of the deputation said that they would welcome such a scheme but another felt that the small shopkeepers, who were in a majority, would petition against the order. This led Mr Churchill to retort, 'Exactly. But that is what I say. It is almost impossible for me to go beyond public opinion. Up to a certain point I can help it and urge it, but if people do not want it, and will not have it, and say they mean to go on, and if the smaller shopkeepers use their weight against the thing, and say they will not have their shops closed on those suggestions, I have not the force to carry it.' Another of the deputation countered this by saying that some years ago they had taken this line in talking to Mr H. Gladstone, the then home secretary, 'but our experience during the last few years has proved the impossibility of getting early closing except by compulsory measures'.

A deputation from the National Union of Shop-Assistants, Warehousemen and Clerks on 4 November said that at the time over a thousand districts, large and small, had a half-holiday, beginning, in over five hundred cases, at 1pm and in the remainder at 2pm. They did not want these gains lost. To this deputation Mr Churchill pointed out that many bodies of traders favoured a universal half-holiday, but when he considered making this compulsory, 'I found the greatest difficulty for this reason: the opposition of the small shopkeepers all over the place was coming in very formidably, and it would make so manifest an amount of resistance to the bill that it might prevent it getting through.' So he was considering getting the Home Office to initiate the machinery in every locality to secure voluntary early closing and making this depend on a two-thirds majority of those voting in a local ballot on the matter. When he was asked what the position of the assistants would be, he replied:

> Every shop-assistant will have his half-holiday absolutely safe-guarded under severe penalties, by the law. You do not know what opposition that is going to get round. I liked the idea of the universal half-holiday, but I began to see and hear of the defence: little traders beginning to be alarmed ... My interests are yours; I want to get you the best bill I possibly can. I would not have touched it except for the sake of the shop-assistant.

After the obvious note of alarm in these various statements at the opposition the idea of a compulsory half-holiday for all shops was causing, it is not surprising to read in *The Times* on 14 November that Mr Churchill had announced that he had decided to withdraw the provision requiring all shops to close for a half-holiday but to reserve the right of every shop-assistant to a half-holiday.[31] The same issue of *The Times* records a demonstration on the previous afternoon—a Sunday—in Trafalgar Square organised by the London branch of the Shop-Assistants' Union. This gave general support to the bill but called for an amendment that the sixty-hour week should be inclusive of meals. Otherwise, as the bill stood the assistants would be doing a seventy-hour week. The assistants also wanted 1pm fixed as the closing hour on half-holidays. One speaker made the significant statement that only five per cent of the male shop-assistants had a vote, and of course no women then had a vote. Undoubtedly here lies the key to some, not all, of the reluctance on the part of successive governments to do anything really positive on the matter of hours worked in shops. On the other hand of course the small shop-keeper was usually a voter, and one who could influence other voters very often, when they were his customers. On the Friday of the same week the prime minister announced that Parliament would be dissolved at the end of the month.

There was published along with the account of the deputations that visited the Home Office about the 1910 bill a return of the closing orders made under the act of 1904.[32] This showed that in England and Wales 271 orders affecting 19,762 shops had been made since 15 August 1904. Of the orders in force on 31 December 1910, only two covered all the traders in a particular place and both these were small places in Devonshire. One of these was Combe Martin, with thirty-seven shops, which all closed at 2pm on Wednesdays, except during July, August and September, when they closed at 6pm. The other was Witheridge with sixteen shops. At Southport, with 690 shops, all but the fishmongers closed for half a day from 1 October to 31 May. But for the other four months they closed at 5pm on man, in opening the debate said that the bill was on the lines of clear that the act of 1904 had achieved very little.

On 6 March 1911 the government re-introduced the Shops' Bill of 1910 and the debate on the second reading took place on 31 March.[33] The under-secretary at the Home Office, Mr Masterman, in opening the debate said that the bill was on the lines of the 1909 bill and proposed a sixty-hour limit for assistants exclusive of meals. Referring to the clause on Sunday closing, he said, 'Of all the questions which have been pressed upon us by deputations representing every class of traders in the country, no question has revealed such unanimity as the desire of the traders for the prevention of the increase of Sunday trading in the country. Sunday provides the shop-assistant with almost the only opportunity for leisure in fresh air.' In his peroration he claimed that if the bill became law it would be 'a social reform which is long overdue', and continued, 'We believe that without any appreciable loss to any trader in the country, and certainly without any decrease in the general consumption of commodities, we may so put pressure upon the public, which is the master of this trade, and which is cruel only because it is careless, that there may be larger opportunities given for efficiency, for leisure, and for happiness among the hundreds of thousands of people to whom these opportunities are at present denied.'

Mr Horatio Bottomley, member for Hackney, led the opposition to the bill claiming that it used unsuitable machinery to try to secure a good object. With the ebullient propensity to make a fraction of the truth represent the whole, which was a notable mark of his career, he claimed that there was no great enthusiasm for the bill among the shop-assistants and he claimed that the home secretary himself was not very enthusiastic. Mr Churchill intervened to state that Mr Bottomley had no right to make such an observation about himself—but if this was not true then, later developments leave one wondering whether here, at any rate, Mr Bottomley was not a truer prophet than was often the case. The real point of Mr Bottomley's opposition was that he posed as the champion of the small shopkeeper against the big stores, and that he considered the phrase 'social reform' mere 'claptrap' used 'to justify the introduction of any degree of parental and officious interference with the habits and avocations of the people'.

Sir Frederick Banbury, member for the City of London, supported Mr Bottomley because the bill would deal with the hours of adult males. In his forthright manner he claimed, 'I am old-fashioned enough still to hold the old Tory belief that if a man chooses to work he ought to be allowed to work as long and as often as he likes'. It was characteristic of him that he took an opposite line to Mr Bottomley on the matter of the opinion of the shop-assistants; he maintained that they were more or less in favour of the bill, 'because they have been captured by the Socialists, who wish to provide for the regulation of everything by the state'.

The exponent of old Toryism did not speak for the Conservative opposition; Mr Lyttleton, on its behalf, supported the bill, admitting that it was necessary because the permissive nature of the act of 1904 had made that law ineffective.

More than one speaker regretted that the compulsory closing of shops had been dropped from the bill but even so the support of the assistants and, too, of members of all parties was claimed for the measure.

In closing the debate Mr Churchill used a sentence which echoes the opinion he had expressed to some of the later deputations to the Home Office: 'The original policy was to proceed by the early closing of shops, and it was only because that was found to be impossible—the counter-resistance was so terrible and obstinate and intractable—that the original policy was abandoned and that we have fallen back as a substitute on the compulsory regulations of the hours of shop-assistants.'

Mr Bottomley could only muster 21 votes against 262 in his opposition to the second reading and one would have expected, therefore, that as a government measure with opposition support its progress would now be uneventful. Unfortunately in its progress through the Standing Committee the bill was very much mutilated.

When it emerged towards the end of July the original clause forbidding the employment of a shop-assistant for more than sixty hours a week (which in itself had not satisfied the assistants who wanted the sixty hours to include, not exclude, meal times) had gone. In its place was a clause saying that no assistant was to be employed after 1.30pm on one day a week. Together with this there was the original clause that every shop, with certain exceptions, was to be closed for the serving of customers by 1pm on one week-day every week. A number of limitations spoilt the full effect of these reforms. For example, the half-holiday was not to be enforced in the week before a Bank or public holiday, or a day of public rejoicing or mourning, if the assistant was not employed on such a day; and it was not to be enforced over a period of four months if the assistant was given two weeks' holiday on full pay in the year. Also the local authority could suspend the half-holiday closing, up to four months in the year, in any holiday resort.

The interval allowed for meals was unsatisfactory, although the enforcement of such an interval was a decided advance. No employee could be engaged for more than six hours without an interval of twenty minutes, and if the period of work included the time from 11.30am to 2.30pm the interval must be forty-five minutes (or one hour if the meal was not taken at the shop), while if the period included the time from 4pm to 7pm an interval of twenty minutes must be allowed (thirty minutes if the meal was not taken at the shop). All regulations about Sunday closing disappeared from the bill—so the old law of 1677 remained as the ineffective check upon general Sunday trading.

The original provision that one seat must be provided for every three women assistants employed in a shop was cut out. But the act of 1899 which dealt with the point remained unrepealed. All the provisions in the original bill for proper ventilation and proper and sufficient sanitary conveniences disappeared.

The bill said the local authorities must appoint inspectors to see that the Shop Acts 1892-1911 were obeyed, and the penalties for breaking the new act would be £1 fine for the first offence, £5 for the second and £20 for the third.

The bill exempted from the weekly half-holiday an unnecessarily long list of shops—these included those selling intoxicating liquor; refreshments; 'motor-cycle and air-craft supplies and accessories to travellers'; newspapers and periodicals; 'meat, fish, milk, cream, bread, confectionery, fruit, vegetables, flowers, and other articles of a perishable nature'; 'tobacco and smokers' requisites'; papers at a railway bookstall; 'medicines and surgical appliances'; 'at an exhibition, if the local authority certify that such retail trade is subsidiary or ancillary only to the main purpose of the exhibition'.

Thus the aim of the Early Closing Association for a weekly half-holiday would be secured but the aims of the Union of Shop-

Assistants, apart from this one valuable result, and the fixing of a period for meals, were not attained.

After the bill had been reported to the House on 20 July it was shelved for months. The government had matters to occupy its attention that it considered far more important than securing even meagre reform for the shopworkers—there was the Insurance Bill, for example, which took a great deal of time, the Parliament Bill, the payment of members, and a Coal Mines Bill, among other business. Then government changes took Mr Churchill away from the Home Office to the Admiralty and replaced him by Mr R. McKenna. It was announced, however, that Mr Churchill would continue to deal with matters connected with the Shops' Bill. The uncertainty in the cabinet about the bill is reflected in an answer of Mr Churchill to the House on 30 October that the government intended to proceed with the bill but still had under consideration whether to include again the clauses to restrict Sunday trading, and the statement of the Prime Minister, Mr H. H. Asquith, on the next day that he could not say when the bill would be taken.

Then on Thursday, 30 November, Mr Churchill told the House that the bill would be considered on Friday, 8 December. In doing so he made a very strange statement—strange coming from such a forceful personality and on behalf of a government that is distinguished for the way it initiated great reforms in the face of strong opposition. He said:

> It has become necessary, if legislation is to go forward at all on the subject, to drop the greater part of the bill. The whole of the Sunday clauses will be dropped, and the whole of the attempt to regulate daily hours of labour of shop-assistants must be dropped. It is not my fault. I can assure honourable gentlemen below the gangway that it is with the very deepest regret that I have felt myself compelled to submit to what is undoubtedly the loss of a portion of the measure to which great importance will be attached in many quarters, but we can, I think, secure certain parts of the bill which will be a real benefit to the large class who are interested in it.

L

He referred to the compulsory half-holiday for assistants and shopkeepers, which he considered affected two million people, and the clause about meal times. He made it clear that suggestions which were in the bill with regard to local authorities fixing a closing hour on other days of the week than the half-holiday, if they were satisfied that the shopkeeper wanted this, would only be continued in the bill if 'the House is in the mood to dispose of them by agreement'.

One can sympathise with a statement made by Mr P. C. Hoffman, a former officer of the Shop-Assistants' Union, with regard to Mr Churchill that, 'if he had shown the same tenacity as his colleague, Mr Lloyd George, did for the Budget, and the same pugnacity to the oppositionist shopkeepers, in Parliament and out, as he used against the railwaymen, then the course of shop-life reform might have been different'.[34] A speaker for the Labour Party, allies of the government, said in the debate that it would have voted against the third reading of the bill, so great was its indignation, but for the union urging support for the bill in order to secure the half-holiday and the compulsory meal-time breaks.[35] Mr Churchill and a Liberal Government could not shake themselves free from the old concepts of laissez-faire where the shopkeeper and the shopping public were concerned. One can hardly picture Mr Churchill as happy in the role of crusader against the businessman—however small his business—and so he had no stomach for the fight. After all, the 'little shopkeepers'— and on 8 December Mr Churchill again referred to the great difficulty the government had to face from them—were voters! Mr Churchill, in the face of the evidence he so well knew, told the House on the same day that if there was to be any relief in the matter of the late hours of shopping 'it must be by the development of voluntary early closing'.

He hoped that the movement for this would be stimulated by a very innocuous clause in the bill. He said, 'It is very melancholy and depressing to notice how very small a proportion of early closing orders have been achieved all over the country', and therefore he was suggesting that the home secretary should appoint somebody to hold an inquiry in any district where the local authority or a large number of shopkeepers and assistants requested this, and if, as a result, an early closing order seemed desirable the home secretary should instruct the local authority to make one.

This clause, therefore, and the bill, as outlined in the form in which it had been re-drafted as described above, became law at the end of 1911 and came into force on 1 May 1912.[36]

The biographer of Sir Charles Dilke, referring to his death in January 1911 and the great loss that was to the cause of shop-workers in the struggle for the whole bill in 1911, wrote: 'many attributed very largely to his absence the fact that the government were obliged to permit mutilation of their proposals before they became law'.[37]

The annual report of the National Union of Shop-Assistants for 1911, referring to the fact that the bill did not come before the House in its last stages until the end of the session, said, 'consequently the government were faced with the alternative of pressing only those points that were non-controversial or of running the risk of the bill being talked out'.[38]

These comments emphasise still further the amazing reluctance of even a progressive, reforming government to act on a matter of such great concern to so many citizens.

The provisions in the act exempting many classes of shops and allowing the suspension of the half-holiday for up to four months in holiday resorts were to cause a lot of uncertainty and many possibilities of evasion. For example, there was correspondence between the borough council of Bexhill-on-Sea, Sussex, and the Home Office about the technical points of a four month suspension order and how proper hours were to be secured. The town wanted the area of the application of the suspension regulations to be within a radius of half a mile from the town centre. The Home Office decided this was unsatisfactory and said that the streets forming the boundary must be named.[39] In Stratford-

upon-Avon the town clerk prosecuted a chemist for selling soap
and tooth powder on the afternoon of the half-holiday only to
lose the case because two local doctors gave evidence that the
ingredients were mentioned in the British *Pharmacopoeia* and
so the articles were medicines.[40]

Hostility to the act led to the formation in London of a 'Shops
Section' to the Insurance Tax Amendment Society, of Chancery
Lane, which distributed handbills and advised inquirers that it
was prepared, for a premium, to provide legal defence and pay
the fines for those prosecuted under the Shop Hours Act. Correspondence in the Home Office files shows that one official felt
that a prosecution of the society for conspiracy would stand a
good chance of success but a higher official decided against this.[41]
Apparently the efforts of the society did not have any serious
consequences but they show the survival of that spirit which had
held up reform for so long.

Except for some enthusiasts, few in authority, in Parliament or
local government, were really prepared to take or to use powers
which would restrict the right of an individual to sell when he
liked or buy when he liked. This seemed to concern the 'liberty'
of the citizen, in a way that restricting the right of the individual
to manufacture when he liked did not. After all, the ordinary
citizen does not go to a factory or a coal-mine to buy something
and so he is not directly concerned if the factory or mine closes
at a certain time. He is concerned if the shop across the street
or at the corner is closed when he expects it to be open. The
manufacturer cannot manufacture alone—he must have employees; the shopkeeper, in many cases, can run his shop alone,
and he did not see why anyone should dictate to him the number
of hours a day he should run it.

It is not the purpose of this book to give a detailed story of the
struggle for earlier closing of shops after 1911. It did not prove
easy to get the local authorities in all areas to enforce the act, as
the annual reports of the National Union of Shop-Assistants
show.[42] World War I was to compel a Coalition Government to

do what the Liberal Government of 1911 had refused to do.

Early in 1916 a serious coal shortage necessitated economies in lighting and heating and on 24 October the home secretary, acting under special war regulations, drafted an order that shops should close by 7pm through the winter months, except on Saturday when they could be open until 9pm.[43] The shopkeepers were, in many cases, finding it difficult or unsatisfactory to keep open for the long hours which had remained customary, because assistants were scarce, people were less inclined to shop late at night in darkened streets, and supplies of goods were less plentiful. Nevertheless, it is significant that in consequence of representations made to the House of Commons the order was changed three days later to one making 8pm the closing hour instead of 7pm. These representations were made on two grounds: first that many thousands of small traders would be ruined by a 7pm closing, and secondly, that large numbers of women munition workers could not complete their shopping by 7pm.

In April 1917 the order was renewed for six months on the grounds that the earlier closing benefited the health of the women and girls, who had replaced the men assistants now in the Forces, and that those men who remained in the shops, as proprietors or assistants, would have more time to cultivate their allotments, or do other work of national importance.

After renewal of the order in September 1917 and April 1918 it was again renewed in September 1918 until further notice. It would have expired, with other war regulations, on 31 August 1920, except for the fact that by then shopkeepers and the public had grown so accustomed to the earlier closing of shops that there was a general desire for a continuation of the control of shop hours. Even the National Federation of Small Traders' Protection Associations, which had said that the first order would ruin the small shopkeepers, urged the government to continue the system. This was done by a temporary act passed in December 1920.[44] As in the original order, certain shops were exempted from the 8pm closing, namely those selling meals; fresh fish or soft fruit which would be unsuitable for food if not sold that day; medicines, in case of necessity; newspapers; bookstalls at main stations; motor or cycle supplies in cases of necessity; and intoxicating liquors.

An act of 19 August 1921 allowed the sale of fruit, table-water, sweets, chocolates and ice-cream until 9.30pm on days of the week other than Saturday, and 10pm on Saturdays.[45] The acts of 1920 and 1921 were renewed annually until 1928.

In March 1927 the House of Commons appointed a Departmental Committee, under the chairmanship of Sir W. W. Mackenzie, to inquire into the working of the acts of 1920 and 1921 and to consider whether they should be made permanent.[46] The conclusions of the committee bore out the claims made, for so many years before 1911, by those who had advocated legislation to impose shorter hours. Shopkeepers had not been ruined and the health of the workers had benefited by earlier hours. For example, the report of the commission said:

> The experience of the last ten years shows that a general closing hour, such as 8pm, has been of great benefit to shop-assistants and shopkeepers. It was stated before us that the general health of shop-assistants had improved, and that they benefited in other ways from being relieved from the great hardship of the long hours which they formerly had to work. We are satisfied that some restrictions are necessary to prevent a return to former conditions, even if they should tend to the detriment of some shopkeepers and to the inconvenience of a section of the shopping public. We are further satisfied that it would be very difficult, if not impossible, to secure these restrictions by voluntary agreement.

In other parts of the report support was given to the conclusions by the evidence which the commission had heard. In a summary of the evidence given by the Early Closing Association, which then claimed 50,000 to 60,000 subscribers, the report said, 'When in 1916 compulsion came the country was found to be ready for it and had in some measure anticipated it, and experience showed that the public had not been inconvenienced.' It added, 'Small shopkeepers welcomed early closing as emancipation from the "shop slavery" which had previously been their lot.'

The National Chamber of Trade, with a membership of 100,000 shopkeepers, was emphatic in approving compulsory closing. In this they were supported by the London and Suburban Traders' Federation with a membership of 10,000, the majority of whom were owners of one-man businesses. This federation was reported as stating, 'no falling off of business as the result of shortened hours had been observed'.

The report stated, with regard to the representative of the National Federation of Shopkeepers and Small Traders' Protection Associations, ninety per cent of whose 5,000 businesses were one-man concerns, that he had

> mentioned that from 1908 to 1918 he was himself a small shopkeeper who kept his shop open from 7am to 11pm on week-days and also opened on Sunday mornings. When the proposal to close shops early in the evening was made he, in common with many thousands of small traders, believed he would be ruined, and did all he could to oppose the order. As the result of actual experience of early closing he had entirely changed his views. The shortening of hours had not led to a reduction in the amount of trade.

The National Amalgamated Union of Shop-Assistants, Warehousemen and Clerks, with a membership of 65,000, was stated in the report to favour the continuation of legislation but to desire that 7pm be the closing hour on four nights and 8pm on the late night. In this they were supported by the National Union of Distributive and Allied Workers, with a membership of 96,000 chiefly in co-operative shops.

An echo of earlier days came from an individual witness, in contrast to those who testified in a representative capacity, Mr F. A. Macquisten, KC, MP, who claimed that the early closing movement was mainly concerned with the interests of the big stores and multiple combines. He maintained that restricted shopping hours prevented assistants starting their own shops. He suggested that complete liberty for the shopkeeper and his family to run a business as they wished would reduce the cost of living.

Another individual witness, Mr H. Becker, who as a member of the House of Commons in 1922-3 had introduced bills to amend the acts of 1920-1, claimed that there was a strong demand by the public and small shopkeepers for unrestricted hours while safeguarding the hours of assistants. He made the old plea that a man who employed nobody should be allowed to open his shop for as long as he wished.

These individuals did not impress the committee and it recommended that 8pm be made by law the closing hour, except on the late day, when it was to be 9pm, and early closing day; though it stated that it knew 'that many shops do in fact close earlier than the hour required by existing legislation'. The act of 1928 put these recommendations into effect with certain reservations on the lines of the original wartime orders and the acts of 1920 and 1921.[47]

The Shops Act of 1934 carried some of the other aims of the pioneers of the earlier days to completion.[48] It said that no young person was normally to be employed for more than forty-eight hours a week. Those between sixteen and eighteen could, however, be employed for longer hours in the case of seasonal or other pressures of work but such overtime must not exceed fifty hours in the year or twelve hours in one week, and must not take place in more than six weeks of any year. The forty-eight hour week became a forty-four hour week for those under sixteen by the Young Persons (Employment) Act of 1938. The act of 1934 also insisted on the provision in shop premises of suitable and sufficient means of ventilation, heating, sanitation, lighting, and proper washing facilities.

The Shops Act of 1950 consolidated the previous legislation.[49] By it the closing hours for the four winter months, November to February, were fixed at 7.30pm on the late day, 1pm on the early closing day, and 6pm on other days. For the rest of the year the hour was 9pm on the late day and 8pm on the days which had been 6pm. A number of shops were exempt from these hours on the lines of previous exemptions. The main points of the other legislation, which we have noted, were repeated. Every shop was to be closed on Sunday, but the full effect of this was spoilt by the too great number of exceptions, especially in holiday resorts.

Thus by 1950 almost all that those who had struggled to obtain a really worth-while standard of hours and conditions for shopworkers in 1911 had desired had been secured. This, as usual, had come about without any of the disasters which the faint-hearted and those bound by out-of-date or false theories had foretold would follow in the wake of legislative compulsion for the half-holiday and early closing.

CHAPTER NINE

CONCLUSIONS

The story of the struggle to obtain shorter working hours and a weekly half-holiday for the shop-assistants and their employers shows that the old concept of laissez-faire died more slowly in Victorian and Edwardian England than those historians, who have fixed their attention almost exclusively upon industrial conditions, have led their hearers or readers to believe. It is important that a more balanced picture should be painted for the assumption has all too often been made that the story of the nineteenth century shows that the public had only to be made aware, by a few enlightened reformers, of the need for some change in bad conditions and its innate goodness would demand and secure the needed reform. This, in turn, helped to maintain the assumption that progress to ideal conditions was inevitable.

The pioneer work of Robert Owen and Lord Shaftesbury—to mention only two names—and the reports of a couple of parliamentary committees led, within not much more than thirty years, to the first really effective Factory Act in 1833. Another committee and some hard work produced the quite drastic Coal Mine Act of 1842. Stout blows at laissez-faire in less than half a century! Yet from the start of the Metropolitan Early Closing

Association, in the same year as that Coal Mine Act, it was to be another forty years before the first committee on conditions in the shops was to be set up. Certainly this committee resulted in legislation affecting young people, but in view of conditions in industry by then, it marked no brave advance in the country's general attitude to its youth. Then in the next fifteen years there were to be three more committees, all reporting the need for reform, and a resolution of the House of Commons in favour of action; and yet nothing was done. Such a repeated proclamation of a need, and such a continuous failure by Parliament to face up to the only possible way to meet the need, is surely without parallel in our history. Yet it is part of our social and economic story entirely ignored in most pictures of the period.

The charge is often made today that this or that political party, or some section of a party, is making a fetish of some doctrinaire point. Many seem to think this is a new feature of political life. The story we have traced should disabuse anyone holding that idea. Neither the Conservative nor the Liberal Party could free themselves from such strange doctrines as that the state must not interfere with a man's hours of work; that the shopkeeper must be at the beck and call of the customer; that nothing must be done to check the right of the individual to make money, provided he appeared to keep within the law.

The support of the great Victorian middle-class population for industrial reforms could be given without these reforms altering the pattern of life of the average supporter. Shorter hours in the coal mine, iron foundry, engineering works or factory did not directly concern the ways of life of many who advocated or supported legislation to obtain these benefits. The country prospered in spite of, if not because of, these changes. So, at no cost or inconvenience to oneself, there was the satisfaction of knowing that a number of one's fellows had had their conditions of life and work improved. Alongside this went the growing power of the workers concerned, organised more and more efficiently, as the century drew to a close, through trade unions.

The picture was very different in the matter of the retail shop. If the shop at which you were accustomed to buy closed at an earlier hour than customary, then your freedom to purchase when you chose was curtailed. Love of freedom—without much consideration for the real meaning and implications of the word—was a great Victorian watchword and any threat to the freedom of the individual, except of course by his employer in the legitimate interests of trade, must be resisted when you were the individual threatened. The shop existed first of all to make as much money as possible for the owner, and secondly for the convenience of the shopping public. The latter included everyone and so consideration for those who worked in shops must be subordinated to the whims of the customers.

Here, then, was a very different situation. The public must be prepared to make personal sacrifices if the necessary reforms were to come, and, as we have seen, most people were not prepared to make such sacrifices. This point is illustrated by the fact that it was easier to secure a half-holiday and earlier hours of closing in the shops which did a high-class trade, because their customers were not really inconvenienced by these changes, than it was in the great number of ordinary shops.

The natural thoughtlessness and selfishness of the individual—two facts which we like to ignore—played a big part in hindering better conditions for the shopworker. We have seen that it was often the very people who had themselves, as industrial workers or the wives of such, benefited from improved working conditions who helped to perpetuate the long hours for shopworkers because they would not make their purchases earlier as long as the shops remained open to a late hour.

As early as 1867, in an interesting account of the life of the ordinary workers, a writer who claimed to be a journeyman engineer devoted a whole chapter to describing the ways in which the working men and their families spent Saturday afternoons and evenings. He said Saturday was the red-letter day in their week and that 'the Saturday half-holiday movement is one of the

most practically beneficial that has ever been inaugurated with
a view to the social improvement of "the masses" '. Then he
made the following comment:

> But there is one aspect of the Saturday half-holiday movement in
> which those sections of the working classes who have benefited
> by it have been weighed and found wanting. They have not as a
> body given the practical aid which, without any inconvenience to
> themselves or their families, they might have done, and which
> as working men they ought to have done, to the extension of the
> movement among the less fortunate sections of their own class.

The writer pointed out that wages were often paid on Friday
night, 'with an express view to facilitating early shopping and
marketing on Saturdays. And yet it is notorious that the late
shopping of the artisan classes is the sole means of keeping
thousands of shops open till eleven and twelve o'clock on Saturday nights.' In consequence, he declares, Saturday is the worst
day of the week for shopworkers, both owners and assistants, who
often have to shop on Sundays as a result. The writer says that
artisans often 'entertain a rather contemptuous opinion of
"counter-skippers" but they should bear in mind that even
counter-skippers are men and brethren' who 'desire and would
enjoy a half-holiday'. He does not expect that the workers who
have a half-holiday could immediately extend the benefit, but
they could do a great deal to further it.[1]

If there was little sign of 'working-class solidarity' throughout
the period it was in part due to the way the ordinary worker was
contemptuous of the shopworker while the shop-assistant did not
regard him or herself as belonging to the 'working classes'.
Obsequious behind the counter, he or she liked to feel superior
to the industrial worker. This, together with the factors of age,
hope of one's own business one day, need to placate one's employer in whose power was the granting of the essential reference,
prevented a strong trade union developing among shop-
assistants and, without this, a valuable factor in securing real
reform was missing.

The feeling of class-distinction was found, also, within the retail trade itself A former tradesman of seventy years ago has told me that then there was a generally acknowledged gradation of shopkeeping society. The butchers, fishmongers and green-grocers came at the bottom of the scale; then the grocers; the drapers and outfitters ranked a little higher; above them came the chemists. Hence the difficulty of getting the shopkeepers to agree to uniformity of hours, or the assistants to combine in one united effort.

The traditions of the shop-assistants' work meant the main-tenance of an appearance of prosperity and well-being. In all but the poorest neighbourhoods, the shop-assistant was apparently well-dressed and evinced a simulated interest in the needs and whims of the customer. It was difficult to conceive that such a person was in as much, or more, need of pity and protection as the dirty, badly clothed person whose picture you might see representative of the typical factory worker or coal miner. If you lived where you actually saw the industrial workers you found it even more difficult. Here was another factor making it far from easy to rouse the public to the need for reform.

We are still inclined to be bemused by the prosperity of the Victorian age and we rightly admire some of the good qualities which helped to produce it, such as hard work, initiative, sound workmanship, honesty; but we often ignore the evils inherent in the worship of money which blighted so much of the period. In this study we have seen that it was not always safe to rely on the word of a shopkeeper who promised to close his shop at an agreed hour. If he felt that he could gain by breaking his word he broke it and kept his shop open. He was one of a small minority in any place but it is noteworthy that his action did not lead to any lessening of his reputation among his customers. They still trusted him to serve them satisfactorily. His rivals felt that if he broke his word they must follow suit. Honesty did not pay, in such a case, and an Englishman's word was not a very reliable bond where early closing was concerned. The evils consequent upon an undue adherence to the merits of competition are, perhaps, nowhere better illustrated than in the story of the shopkeeper in the nineteenth and early twentieth centuries.

In an earlier chapter a suggestion by Edward Flower of Liverpool that the supply of shops exceeded demand and so led to fierce competitions was noted. Almost certainly this was true throughout the period and it must be kept in mind in any attempt to understand the willingness of the small shopkeeper to keep his shop open at any time when he might secure a customer. If your only hope of survival lay in tempting customers away from a rival, knowing that there was really no justification for the existence of you both, you could not afford to be scrupulous.

We have not outlived some of the attitudes that have been noted. When, from 1950, a number of shops in the West End of London extended their times for closing on one night a week, few of the shopping public inquired whether the interests of the assistants had been safeguarded or whether they were being compensated for the extra time worked. An extra hour could not be added as easily to the working day of a factory worker or coal miner. There is a growing demand, in some places, for all restrictions to be removed from the above hours when shops can be open, on week-days and Sundays. The closer connection of this country with European customs will increase this. Usually the people advocating change on these lines give little thought to the shopworkers and, even if it be assumed that the law will protect the assistants, what will be the position of the shopkeeper who runs his shop alone, or assisted by his wife? Today it only requires one tobacconist or owner of a sweet shop to decide to stay open for part of Sunday, albeit illegally, for competitors in the vicinity to follow suit.

That these things can be, shows how blind to some of the elements in human nature those who advocated the principle of voluntaryism were. Voluntary action had an important part to play in showing what might be done to improve the conditions of the shopworker but it was insufficient to master the problem.

Legislation was a necessary ally whose aid should have been enlisted long before it was.

The story that has been traced illustrates another feature of Victorian society, namely the apathy of the churches, as institutions, to social problems and the zeal of individual churchmen, with a wider vision of their Christian responsibilities, in the cause of reform. Over and over again ministers of religion of varying denominations were prominent in denouncing from platform or pulpit the evils of the system of long shop hours and advocating more humane conditions. Church assemblies were normally silent. The very respectableness of Victorian religion tied its hands when making money was also a sign of respectability. When prosperity in business was taken as the providential reward of the Christian virtue of hard work it was almost blasphemous to suggest that you might be committing sin in forcing, by your example or your power, a competitor, or a recipient of your custom, or an employee, to work too hard. Rather than come to grips with that proposition it was better to find virtue in the way long hours of business prevented opportunity for vice.

We have seen that there were many in the period who saw that if the claims of Christianity were to be brought to the notice of the individual, and if Sunday were to be observed as a day of rest and worship, it was essential to see that adequate time was given for recreation, through sport and amusement and leisure pursuits, on some other day of the week. The advocate of proper Sunday observance was often the champion of a shorter working week. It has also to be noted that many professing Christians, who were shopkeepers, did not allow any Christian regard for the well-being of their employees to interfere with the overriding claims of business. In many cases this was so because little thought had ever been given to the application of Christian principles to the working condition of employees. In other cases the pretence was made that they were doing a Christian service to their employees by keeping them occupied for long hours because otherwise the employees would have misused their leisure. This illustrated the Victorian aptitude for rationalising some condition which it would have been inconvenient to change.

There is still much to be discovered, recorded and interpreted before a complete picture of the Victorian age is available. In such a picture quite a large space will be occupied by the shop-keeper and his assistant. More material than has yet been available for this part of the picture needs to be gleaned from local records of individual businesses and societies, and from diaries and account books. More local research needs to be made into the minutes of early closing associations, where they still exist,[2] or the columns of local papers in order to produce this material.

By way of showing how local sources illustrate the main trends of the present study, the next chapter, a postscript, traces something of the story of the efforts to obtain the earlier closing of shops in one town. Here, only a few years before this inquiry was started, the minutes of the local early closing association had been destroyed as not likely to be of any further use. I talked with one who was the secretary at the turn of the century. He was then in his eighties and it was almost impossible to verify some of his recollections, valuable as they were for local colour. In the main the story has had to be put together from the files of local newspapers. I hope others may be fortunate enough to see, and use, minute books which must contain interesting information about a not unimportant side of the everyday life of the community.

M

CHAPTER TEN

POSTSCRIPT

The Efforts to Secure Early Closing and a Half-Holiday by Voluntary Means in Gravesend, Kent, 1879-1913

The first attempt to secure any alteration in shop hours by united action in the borough of Gravesend was made on Wednesday, 4 June 1879, when the mayor, at the request of a number of tradesmen and assistants, called a meeting to consider the closing of shops at 5pm on Wednesday during the summer.[1] The meeting was attended by Mr F. S. Allen from the London Early Closing Association. 'He was told that in Gravesend it was not uncommon for assistants to work thirteen and fourteen hours per day, and on Saturdays even more than that, their labours extending into Sunday morning.' A grocer, Mr T. Smith, said that he had tried, unsuccessfully, to get other grocers to join him in closing at 5pm on Wednesdays, two years before. He had closed his own shop, 'and did not think he had lost anything by it'. An ironmonger, Mr M. H. Bevan, said that in the previous winter all the ironmongers had closed at 7pm except on Saturday. The motion, which these two proposed and seconded, for a Wednesday 5pm closing was carried unanimously. The outcome of the meeting was the formation of an association to promote the work thus indicated and in commenting on this the leading article of the

local paper on 14 June said that the neighbouring towns of
Maidstone and Dartford already closed at 5pm on Wednesdays.

To begin with a number of shops fell into line but complete
uniformity was not obtainable because two or three drapers were
accustomed to close at 5pm on Saturdays, which enabled their
assistants to get away for the Sunday, and they did not propose
to change to Wednesday; also one of the shops, dealing in oil and
colours, refused to close and so the other shops doing similar
business threatened to stay open as well. Still, by late July the
local association contained fourteen honorary members, twenty-
one tradesmen and 150 assistants, and over eighty had had an
evening excursion on Wednesday, 30 July, in waggonettes to a
local beauty spot where they had danced in the woods to the
music of a violin and harp.[2]

In the winter an effort was made to secure the closing of shops
at 8pm, except on Fridays and Saturdays, but this came to
nothing.[3] The local society had as its secretary Mr Albert Larking,
who was later to be a prominent official of the parent society,
and who was responsible for the calling of the meeting on 4 June.
In the summer of 1880 arrangements were once more made for a
Wednesday 5pm closing. The rector of Milton Parish, with the
borough, and the Presbyterian minister were persuaded to preach
sermons supporting the idea.[4] One of the leading drapers, Mr
Henry Simmonds, wrote a letter to the local paper, explaining
that he intended to keep open late on Wednesday; he had taken
£20 between 5pm and 8pm the previous Wednesday, and he
gave each employee three hours for recreation each week, which
was doing more than an early closing at 5pm for four months
secured. He struck the note that was to make havoc so often of
schemes for co-operation, writing, 'But, sir, it is just as well that
it should be known through your paper, that we are independent
both of the plaudits and sneers of neighbours. Our business is
carried on in our own way, and we enjoy that position in the
town, which will not allow us to be dictated to by any clique as
to what time we shall close.'[5]

A later letter pointed out that others would follow Mr Simmonds in not closing without giving their assistants the three hours free that he gave, and expressing surprise that 'a philanthropic gentleman of his broad views and experience' could not see the benefit of the uniform closing.[6] It seemed as if, in this case, wiser counsel had prevailed for at the annual meeting of the association on 13 July Mr Herbert Simmonds said that 'he and his father were willing to close at any time, even for a half-day or a whole day, if others would do the same'.[7] Even so this qualification was a safeguard and is still symptomatic of the weakness underlying the voluntary effort.

Suggestions were made in that July meeting for the 5pm Wednesday closing to become permanent throughout the year. This seems to have come to nothing for the local paper on 14 April 1883 commented on the apathy in Gravesend on the subject of early closing and expressed the hope that the town would not be behind hand in adopting the Wednesday 5pm closing in the coming summer. On the suggestion of Mr Larking, who was resigning the secretaryship to become assistant secretary to the London association, shop-assistants were to canvass the employers to try to secure the 5pm closing.[8]

In May, Mr Larking was writing in the local paper, 'Ladies are earnestly asked to make their purchases before seven, or at the latest 8 o'clock in the evening, and before 5 o'clock on Wednesdays.'[9] The same pathetic hope that the public would exercise self-discipline on behalf of their fellows is thus seen again. Very familiar, too, is the report, made at a committee of the local association on 23 May, that while the boot trade, clothiers and hosiers have agreed to the 5pm Wednesday closing, 'the grocers remained open through the action of two, who declined to close until the drapers closed. It was also regretted that the drapers refused to close owing to two firms closing on Saturday, that day being more convenient to them'.[10] Judging from a later reference Mr Simmonds did not close after all, but 'We have made arrangements by which one assistant will leave business every day at 2 o'clock, so ensuring, as we think, a reasonable recreation.'

One can sympathise with the two drapers who refused to change from their system of 5pm closing on Saturdays which they had followed for thirteen years, but at the same time one can see how their action gave a loophole for others to refuse to close on Wednesdays. One member of the association at a general meeting on 28 May commented that those who refused to close at 5pm were all prominent members of churches and chapels and that although they were very particular about the welfare of people's souls they denied their assistants opportunities of fresh air for a few hours a week.[11]

In June a Congregational minister preached a sermon, in support of the association, in which he appealed to the public not to shop late, saying that when they prayed for those who absented themselves from worship, because of the long hours of work in the week, 'they should think whether they had thoughtlessly done aught to prevent the absent ones from being present by adding to their hours of labour through late shopping'. However, the Rev T. F. Touzeau rejected any idea of legislative aid. 'What did not touch the public mind by moral suasion would not stand any length of time by force.'[12]

On the other hand another Congregational minister in the town, the Rev E. Bolton, said in September that only legislation would achieve what was required.[13] In October it was reported that the ironmongers and clothiers had decided to close at 5pm on Wednesdays throughout the year.[14]

The local paper, in November, seemed to think that, as the association 'is supported by all right thinking persons', it was assured of quick success.[15] But almost at once silence descended —the association seemed to fade out—and by 1888 one would imagine that all ideas of an early Wednesday closing had been forgotten, for when a philanthropic lady provided a free tea for over a hundred shop lads it had to be held at 8pm on a Wednesday.[16]

A fresh start was made in the spring of 1890 when a new

local early closing association was formed which, by November, had nearly a hundred members. By then it was claimed that 'early closing on Wednesdays is now practically universal', but what was meant by the statement is shown by the further appeal to the public to ensure success, 'by making their purchases before 4 o'clock on Wednesdays'.[17] The old difficulties cropped up again. At a meeting in January 1891 it was reported that two tradesmen kept open until 7pm on Wednesdays because they were accustomed to close at 5pm on Saturdays and this was used as an excuse for others to remain open on Wednesdays beyond 4pm.[18] However, ten days later the local paper carried this news item about early closing:

> We are glad to find that this movement continues to be observed, and in order to render it of a permanent character Messrs Bryant and Rackstraw and Mr Plummer announce, by advertisement, that their establishments will be closed on Wednesday evenings, in addition to Saturday evenings. The liberal concessions made by these firms will be appreciated by all well-wishers of early closing.[19]

In October 1892 the association was considering the possibility of making the hour of closing 2pm on Wednesday but not all the eighty-nine members favoured this.[20] In any case closing at 4pm was not universal yet. The subject was still under consideration two years later, when many felt that it was more important to work for earlier closing on other evenings of the week. It was still exceptional for a shop to close by 8pm.[21]

The local association nearly died in October 1895,[22] and although it continued to exist its effort to secure an earlier hour for closing each evening evidently met with no success because, in January 1896, a social evening arranged for a Tuesday was fixed to start at 9pm, 'in consequence of the shops not closing earlier'.[23] The Wednesday closing at 4pm was now fairly well observed; the boot shops had tried to get a 2pm closing and had failed, but at least one tailor closed at that hour and three grocers. The local paper commented on the fact that out of an estimated

400 to 500 young shop-assistants in the town only about eighty belonged to the association.

The opinion was expressed at the annual meeting of the association in 1897 that it was two or three in each trade who prevented a 2pm closing. The local paper said that many trades-men would prefer earlier closing on other evenings to the 2pm on Wednesdays and added, 'We certainly think this would be the better course for all concerned, as their assistants would have the opportunity of attending entertainments and other means for healthful enjoyment and improvement.'[24] However, by 1898 the 2pm closing was generally observed.

The struggle for earlier hours continued without success until the early winter of 1901 when the association announced that, from January to April inclusive in 1902, a large number of shop-keepers would close at 8pm on Mondays, Tuesdays and Thurs-days.[25] We are left to surmise at what hour shops closed on Friday and Saturday nights. This 8pm closing either broke down, or was not renewed, for in February 1904 the secretary of the association, in his report for 1903, said that it was only in November 1903 that the clothing, jewellery, boot and drapery trades agreed to the 8pm closing. From other remarks which he made it is clear that the early closing on Wednesday was again not everywhere observed.[26]

The local Tradesmen's Association, in co-operation with the local Early Closing Association, decided in October 1904 to work to secure the application of the Shop Hours Act in Gravesend. If the necessary support was secured the hours which it was sug-gested that the town council should fix were: Monday, Tuesday, Thursday, 8pm; Wednesday, 1pm; Friday, 9pm; Saturday, 11pm.[27] This does not seem to have succeeded for, by April 1905, the report of the annual meeting of the Early Closing Association said that it was attended by only a few members and that the chairman expressed the need to canvass the town in favour of applying the act, adding, 'It would indeed be a great pity were they to lose the two o'clock movement, and it rested entirely with the shop-assistants themselves.'[28] No closing order under the act had been secured for Gravesend by the end of 1910.[29]

That it remained impossible to get all the shops to close on Wednesday afternoon is shown by the Return of Closing Orders under the 1911 act. There Gravesend appeared in the list of places where the order for the half-holiday closing was to apply to certain classes of shops and not all shops. The shops listed were grocers, boot dealers, drapers, outfitters, barbers, jewellers, ironmongers, photographers, oilmen, stationers, dealers in coal, china ware, leather goods, furniture, corn. This totalled 370 shops, and must have included almost all the shops, so that we can conclude that, if not officially, in general the Wednesday half-holiday had become the rule by 1913.[30]

NOTES

Chapter 1

1 Flower, Edward. *Hours of Business*, 1843, 7, 8, 9. See also Landels, Wm. *English Slavery and Early Closing*, 1856, 10, 12

2 Ablett, William. *A Few Every Day Hints addressed to the Youths and Young Men of the Drapery Trade*, 2nd ed 1856, 4, 12

3 Anon. *The Shopkeepers Guide*, 1853, 164-5, 55. See also *The Handy Book of Shopkeeping*, 1866

4 The *Early Closing Advocate*, March 1854, 39; April 1854, 58

5 The *Social Science Review*, ed B. W. Richardson, MD, vol 11, 1864, 213, 214

6 *Wesleyan Methodist Magazine*, February 1873, 181-3

7 Sutherst, Thomas. *Death and Disease Behind the Counter*, 1884, 225

8 Grindrod, R. B. *The Wrongs of our Youth*, 1843, 27-8

9 Landels, William. *English Slavery and Early Closing*, 1856, 13, 14

10 Hollingshead, John. *Ways of Life*, 1861, 245-8

11 The *Lancet*, January to June 1851, 72, 21, and 470, 103, 144, 162, 344, 423; July-October, 42-3, 213, 324

12 Harrison, J. F. C. *The Early Victorians 1832-51*, 1971, 68

13 Report from the Select Committee on the Shop Hours Bill, 16 June 1892, 245-8; see also for Sunday living-in conditions, Booth, Charles. *Life and Labour of the People in London*, vol VII, 1896, 75-6

14 Anderson, Will. *The Counter Exposed*, 1896, 37-9, 53, 84

15 The *Daily Chronicle*, 4 February 1898, 5; 10 February, 5; 17 February, 7; 24 February, 4; 5 March, 3; 10 March, 8; 17 March, 7; 24 March, 7; 31 March, 3; 7 April, 7. Also other articles in various issues in April and May

16 *Behind the Counter, Sketches by a Shop-Assistant*, 1888, 11

17 *The Warehousemen and Drapers' Trade Journal*, 21 February 1891, 152

18 Annual Reports of the National Union of Shop-Assistants, 1st Report 1892, *Shop Life Reform, the Recognised Organ of the NSAU*, 18 February 1891 to 8 July 1891, especially 5

19 Report from the Select Committee on the Shop Hours Bill, 1892, 173-82

20 Op cit, 11 above

21 *Shop Life and its Reform*, Fabian Tract no 90, 1897, 12

22 Bondfield, Margaret. *A Life's Work*, 32, 49, 62, 29

23 Reports of NUSA, 8th Report, 1898

24 Op cit, 19 above

25 Op cit, 12 above, 28-9, 45, 62-3

26 Op cit, 13 above, 4 February 1898, 5

27 Report of the Truck Committee, vols 1-3, 1908; vol 4, 1909; III, 119

28 Op cit, III, 139-40

29 Op cit, III, 124, 129, 135, 124, 125, 137

30 Op cit, III, 216

31 Op cit, III, 192

32 Op cit, III, 207

33 Op cit, III, 314

34 Op cit, III, 329-32, 351, 344

35 Op cit, III, 125

36 Op cit, III, 154

37 Op cit, III, 146-53

38 Black, Clementine. *Sweated Industry and the Minimum Wage*, 1907, 60-61, 63, 64. Additional material to illustrate conditions at the end of the nineteenth century and in the early years of the twentieth century is given in *They Also Serve—the Story of the Shopworker*, by Hoffman, P. C., published in 1949. Mr Hoffman writes of his own experiences when living in and of some of the evidence given to the Departmental Committee on the Truck Acts. Information of a similar character is found in Hallsworth, Joseph, and Davies, Rhys J., *The Working Life of Shop-Assistants*, 1910. See also Cadbury, Edward, and others, *Women's Work and Wages*, 1906

39 Smith, Albert. *Sketches of London Life and Character*, 1859, 117

40 *Punch*, 30 June 1860, 258

41 *Chambers' Journal*, 15 October 1864, 670

42 Wynter, Andrew. *Our Social Bees*, 1861

43 Greville, Lady Violet. *Faiths and Fashions*, 1880, 248-9

44 Hobsbawm, E. J. *Industry and Empire* (Pelican Economic History of Britain, vol 3), 1969, 163; Adburgham, Alison. *Shops and Shopping*, chapter XIII, 1964

45 The *Fortnightly Review*, vol 57, January 1895, 124

46 Op cit, 128

47 Op cit, 131

48 Greig, Mrs David. *My Life and Times*, 1940

Chapter 2

1 The *Liverpool Monthly Magazine*, December 1838, 10

2 Flower, E. *Hours of Business*, 1843, 3

3 Op cit, 4, 16, 30, 34, 35

4 Fourth Annual Report of the Liverpool Association of Assistant Tradesmen, 1844, 9, 10

5 *The Times*, 18 August 1825

6 *The Times*, 20 August 1825

7 *The Times*, 24 August 1825

8 Philanthropos, *The Linen Drapers' Magna Charta*, 1839

9 Rules of the Metropolitan Drapers' Association, 1842

10 See article in the *London Quarterly and Holborn Review* for October 1949

11 Minutes of Wesleyan Methodist Conference, 1844, 129

12 Davies, Thomas. *Prize Essay on the Evils which are produced by Late Hours of Business*, 1843, 2. See also 3, 10, 12, 24, 28. For similar information see King, A. J. *The System of Late Hours in Business*, 1843, 25; and Willcock, H. D. (ed) *Browns and Chester*, 1947, 118

13 Op cit, III-VIII

14 Third Annual Report of the Liverpool Association of Assistant Tradesmen, 1844, 16, 17

15 Op cit, 10; and A Verbatim report of the Fifth Annual Meeting of the Metropolitan Early Closing Association, 17 March 1847; also *The Times*, 18 March 1847, 7

16 *The Times*, 27 November 1843, 3

17 *The Times*, 10 February 1844, 5

18 *The Times*, 12 November 1845

19 *The Times*, 3 December 1845

20 *The Times*, 19 December 1845

21 *The Times*, 17 January 1846

22 The *Evangelical Magazine*, January 1845, 33-4

23 A Verbatim report of the Fifth Annual Meeting of the Metropolitan Early Closing Association, 17 March 1847; also *The Times*, 18 March 1847, 7

24 Report of Sixth Annual Meeting, 6, 14

25 *Illustrated London News*, 29 January 1848, 52

26 *The Times*, 14 November 1844, 6; 29 November, 5

27 Lilwall, J. *The Half-Holiday Question*, 2nd edn, 1856, 132. See also Hammond, J. L. and B. *The Age of the Chartists*, 1930, 348

28 *The Times*, 2 September 1848, 7

29 *The Times,* 8 September 1849, 5

30 Arthur, William. *The Successful Merchant,* 1852, 213, 217

31 See Clark, G. Kitson. *The Making of Victorian England,* 1962, 43, 45; Briggs, Asa. *The Age of Improvement,* 1959, chapter 8

Chapter 3

1 Taylor, J. R. *Government, Legal and General Saturday Half-Holiday,* 4th edn, 1857, 19, 22, 27, 85-7, etc

2 Miller, James. *Labour Lightened not Lost,* 1856

3 'Ten Years' Subscriber', Remarks on the Last Address from the Committee of the Metropolitan Drapers' Association to the Assistants of the Metropolis and its suburbs, 1855

4 Fitzgerald, John. *The Duty of Procuring More Rest for the Labouring Classes; the earlier closing of shops, and the Saturday Half-Holiday,* 1856, 21-2

5 Op cit, 69

6 The *York Herald,* 23 September, 14 October 1854

7 FitzGerald, op cit, 74

8 Lilwall, John. *The Half-Holiday Question,* 2nd edn, 1856, 8

9 Op cit, 26

10 Op cit, 27

11 Op cit, 5

12 Op cit, 18

13 Anonymous. *Saturday Half-Holidays and the Earlier Payment of Wages,* 3; also 4, 11, 12, 20, 21 24, 30

14 *The Times,* 11 September 1856

15 *The Times,* 2 March 1853

16 *The Times,* 25 March 1853; see also Wallace, Rev Thomas. *British Slavery*

17 *The Times,* 28 March 1853

18 *The Times*, 31 March 1853

19 Minutes of Evidence taken before the Select Committee (House of Lords), 22 June 1855, 1-4, 15, 25, 38, 42

20 *The Times*, 17 August 1857

21 Practical Testimonies to the Benefits attending the Early Payment of Wages etc, by the Early Closing Association, 1858; and *The Times*, 12 August 1859

22 The *York Herald*, 16 September 1854. The *Yorkshireman*, 16 September, 14 October 1854. The *Yorkshire Gazette*, 16 September 1854

23 *The Necessity of Early Closing to Self-Culture*. Two Prize Essays by Smeeton, William and Davis, Harry J. 1855, 6, 14

24 *The Times*, 22 January 1852, 7

25 *The Times*, 2 March 1853

26 Dennis, John. *The Pioneer of Progress*, 1860, 76, 81, 110-13

27 *The Times*, 7 June 1860, 12

28 *Punch*, 11 August 1860, 53

29 Graves, Charles L. *Mr Punch's History of Modern England*, vol I, 1841-57, 1921, 38

30 *Punch*, 7 September 1861, 99

31 Public Tribute to Mr John Lilwall, 1858

Chapter 4

1 *Draper and Clothier*, July 1859, 88, 89

2 Op cit, 97, 98

3 Op cit, September 1859, 144

4 Op cit, October 1859, 175

5 Op cit, 176

6 Op cit, December 1859, 226, and January 1860, 252

7 Op cit, October 1860, 128

8 *The Times*, 3 December 1864

9 *The Times*, 29 November 1865

10 *The Times*, 5, 7 etc November 1866

11 *The Times*, 4 August 1866

12 *The Times*, 1 December 1869

13 *The Times*, 1 May 1872

14 Hansard, Parliamentary Debates 1886, vol 12 January to 4 March, 683

15 *The Times*, 23 May 1878, 5

16 *The Times*, 12 May 1879, 5

17 *The Times*, 9 June 1882, 8

18 *The Times*, 22 January 1883, 9

19 *The Times*, 19 January 1883, 7

20 *The Times*, 25 January 1883, 7

21 *The Times*, 29 May 1884

22 *The Times*, 16 January 1885, 6

23 *The Times*, 18 June 1885, 7

24 *The Times*, 29 April 1871, 7; 1 May 1872, 5

25 *Capital and Labour*, no 15, 3 June 1874, 320, 321

26 Jevons, W. S. *The State in Relation to Labour*, 81-4

27 Report from the Select Committee on Shop Hours Regulation Bill, 18 May 1886, 78-84

28 Annual Report of ECA for 1889, title page, 9, 28, 30, 34

29 Annual Report of ECA for 1891, 8, 14

30 Report of Select Committee on the Shop Hours Bill, 1892, 155; *The Times*, 17 November, 19 November, 21 November, 2 December 1892

Chapter 5

1 The *Annual Register*, 1871, Chronicle, 81

2 *Illustrated London News*, 1871, 19 August, 167

3 Hutchinson, Horace G. *Life of Sir John Lubbock, Lord Avebury*, 1914, vol 1, 133-4. See also articles by Smart, E. in *History Today*, December 1971

4 Op cit, Hutchinson

5 Hansard, Parliamentary Debates, 1873, vol March-May, 215; *The Times*, 13 May 1873, 6; Duff, Hon Mrs A. Grant. *Life and Work of Lord Avebury 1834-1913*, 1924, 40

6 *The Times*, 9 June 1873, 11

7 *The Times*, 14 June 1873. See also *Capital and Labour*, 3 June 1874

8 *The Times*, 1 July 1880, 6

9 Bill to Regulate the Hours of Labour in Shops ... in Liverpool, May 1884. Parliamentary Debates 1884, vol April, May, 287

10 Bill 1884, Factory Acts (Extension to Shops). *The Times*, 30 October 1884, 3

11 *The Times*, 13 August 1885, 10. Hutchinson's *Life of Lubbock*, vol 1, 217

12 Bill to Limit the Hours of Labour of Children and Young Persons in Shops, 22 January 1886, Parliamentary Debates January-March 1886, 679-88, 1662

13 Report from the Select Committee on Shop Hours Regulation Bill, 18 May 1886, pp II to VIII of committee's report

14 Op cit, evidence, 15-18

15 Op cit, 19-23

16 Op cit, 224

17 Op cit, 37-9

18 Op cit, 45-9

19 Op cit, 104, 177, 208, 209, 221, 185

20 Op cit, 89-90

21 Op cit, 155-6

22 Op cit, 165

23 Op cit, 76

24 Op cit, 107-9

25 Op cit, 118-23

26 Op cit, 124-30

27 Op cit, 150, 151

28 Op. cit, 179, 180

29 Op cit, 250, 251

30 For examples, op cit, 67-8; 59, 76, 97, 132, 150, 155, 244, 245, 250

31 Op cit, 63

32 Op cit, 91, 92

33 Op cit, 173

34 Op cit, 46-8

35 Op cit, 93-5

36 Op cit, 125

37 Op cit, 224

38 Op cit, 232

39 Op cit, 245-7

40 Op cit, 11-15, 24-35

41 Op cit, 78-84

42 Hutchinson, H. C. Op cit, vol 1, 224; a 'Shop Assistant', *Behind the Counter*, 1886, 12; *The Times*, 19 April 1886, 8

43 Report from the Select Committee on Shops (Early Closing) Bill, 21 May 1895, 1

44 *The Times*, 20 April 1886, 12

45 *The Times*, 16 April 1886, 10

N

46　49 and 50, Vict. C.55

47　Bill to regulate the Hours of Labour in Shops, 26 August 1886

48　*The Times*, 5 January 1886, 11

Chapter 6

1　*The Times*, 26 September 1881, 9

2　*The Times*, 2 May 1882, 5

3　*The Times*, 30 May 1882, 7. For earlier meetings and suggestions about a trade union see *The Times*, 22 November 1881, 11; and 5 December 1881, 6

4　*The Times*, 28 November, 4

5　Sutherst, Thomas, *Death and Disease Behind the Counter*, 1884, V, 3, 9-10, etc

6　Op cit, 73-7, 89, 88

7　*The Times*, 19 January 1883, 7; also for earlier references, 1 January, 7; 3 January, 9

8　*The Times*, 5 February 1883, 7

9　*The Times*, 13 February 1885, 12

10　*The Times*, 19 June 1885, 9

11　Shop Hours Regulation, Correspondence between the Earl of Wemyss and T. Sutherst, Esq, published by Central Office of Liberty and Property Defence League, 1885

Chapter 7

1　Bill to provide for the earlier closing of shops and to make further provision with respect to trading on Sunday, no 99 for 1887

2　*The Times*, 9 March 1887, 7

3　*The Times*, 20 February 1888, 8; 29 February, 8; *Annual Register*, 21 of the Chronicle, 1888

4　51 and 52 Vict. C.38

5 Shops (Weekly Half-Holiday), a bill to enable local authorities to establish a weekly half-holiday for shops, 1889. *The Times*, 7 March 1889, 13

6 *The Times*, 11 March 1889, 10

7 *The Times*, 12 March 1889, 12

8 *The Times*, 18 March 1889, 6

9 *The Times*, 3 March 1890, 10. Bill to enable local authorities to establish a weekly half-holiday for shops, 13 February 1890

10 *The Times*, 27 February, 7

11 Bill to give salaried shop-assistants, male and female, one half-holiday in each week, without closing the shop, 25 March 1890

12 *The Times*, 15 October 1887, 6

13 *The Times*, 10 April 1890, 14

14 *The Times*, 14 March 1890, 3

15 Bill to amend the law relating to the employment of women and young persons in shops, 10 February 1892. Parliamentary Debates 4th series, vol 1, for 1892

16 Report from the Select Committee on the Shop Hours Bill, 16 June 1892, ii, iii
Evidence of Hardern, 208-17
    „   „ Barker, 1-8
    „   „ Johnson, 174
    „   „ Lakeman, 25-6
    „   „ Cornes, 73-5; also see Appendix 1 of this study
    „   „ King, 127-8

17 55 and 56 Vict. C.62. An act to amend the law relating to the employment of young persons in shops, 28 June 1892

18 Parliamentary Debates, vol X for 1893, 14 March-10 April, 237

19 Op cit, 731-64

20 Parliamentary Debates, 4th series, vol XXX, 1895, 316, 1179. Bill no 48

21 Report from the Select Committee on Shops (Early Closing) Bill, 21 May 1895, Reports for 1895, XII. Evidence of Stacey, 1-13
Evidence of Horsman, 14-20

22 Brockway, Fenner. *Socialism over Sixty Years, the Life of Jowett of Bradford*, 35-6

23 Committee of 1895, Report op cit, 50-1

24 Op cit, 60-72

25 Op cit, 105

26 Op cit, 190-8

27 Op cit, 240

28 56 and 57 Vict. C.67; 58, Vict. C.5

29 Booth, Charles. *Life and Labour of the People in London*, vol VII, 'Tailoring Trade', 11; 'Drapers', 67; 'Early Closing Movement', 78; 'Hosiers', 81; 'Butchers', 200; 'Grocers', 217

30 *The Times*, 11 May, 18; 14 May, 16; 15 May, 12; 18 May, 8; 21 May, 5; 26 May, 10; 3 June, 4; 6 June, 8; 4 September, 6; 5 September, 10; 10 September, 11; 12 September, 6

31 Bill for earlier closing of shops, 14 February 1896. Bill to provide that all shop-assistants shall have one half-holiday in each week, 28 April 1896. Bill to amend the law relating to shops, 4 August 1896

32 Op cit, bills 1896, 4 August, Annual Reports of the National Union of Shop-Assistants, 6th Report, 1897, 2. The *Shop-Assistant*, no 3, September 1896

33 *Tomorrow*, July 1896, 34 and 35

34 62 and 63 Vict. C.21. An act to provide for seats being supplied for the use of shop-assistants

35 *The Times*, 1899, 9 June, 3; 23 June, 12; 21 June, 4

36 *The Times*, 1898, 8 December, 8; 10 December, 10; 14 December, 6

37 *The Times*, 13 May 1899

38 See reference in the *Daily Chronicle*, 1898, 12 May, 3

39 *The Times*, 23 March

40 *The Times*, 14 June, 3

41 *The Times*, 24 March 1900, 3

Chapter 8

1 Hansard, Parliamentary Debates, vol LXXXIX, 1st vol for session 1901, 1168-71

2 Ryan, A. P. 'The Marquis of Salisbury', article in *History Today*, April 1951

3 Report of the Select Committee of the House of Lords on Early Closing of Shops, 17 August 1901. Report itself, v-vii
Evidence of Miss Octavia Hill, 13
     „   „ G. Snafe, 37-8
     „   „ J. B. Redfern, 38
     „   „ C. L. Abraham, 89
     „   „ H. Evans, 54
     „   „ J. A. Stacey, 6
     „   „ Rev F. J. W. Horsley, 156
     „   „ Miss N. Vynne, 206
     „   „ Sir J. B. Maple, 45-53
Statement of Avebury about opposition to bill, 87
Evidence of J. Parker, 98-9
     „   „ C. Thompson, 99-100
     „   „ H. Davison, 103-5
     „   „ C. L. Abraham, 87-8
     „   „ J. Williams, 78-9
     „   „ A. Spencer, 19-21

4 A bill to amend the law relating to shops, 19 February 1901

5 *The Times*, 15 March 1901, 10

6 *The Times*, 12 April 1901, 4

7 *The Times*, 16 April 1901, 5

8 *Annual Register 1902*, part 1, 63; also see 1900, part 1, 121. Parliamentary Debates 1902, vol 103, 314-36

9 Parliamentary Debates 1903, vol CXVIII, 17 February to 5 March, 1453-75

10 Shops (Early Closing) (HL) brought from the Lords and ordered by the House of Commons to be printed 18 June 1903. *Annual Register 1903*, part 1, 43-4

11 Parliamentary Debates, op cit, 259, and *Annual Register*, op cit

12 13th Annual Report of the National Union of Shop-Assistants for 1903. *The Times*, 20 June 1903, 16

13 *The Times*, 30 March 1904, 10

14 Parliamentary Debates 1904, vol CXXXIV, 577-606

15 4 Edw. 7, C.31, an act to provide for the early closing of shops

16 14th Report of the NUSA, 3-4
The Times, 21 January 1905, 8

17 *The Times*, 24 January 1905, 16

18 Parliamentary Debates 1907, vol CLXXIII, 960-75

19 Return of Closing Orders made by Local Authorities under Shop Hours Act 1904, published 1909

20 *Annual Register 1906*, part 1, 43, 1907; part 1, 52

21 A bill to provide for the closing of shops and the prohibition of street trading on Sunday, 31 March 1909

22 The *Shopkeeper*, no 1, September 1908, 3; November, 4, 6; March, 10, 12

23 A bill to amend the law relating to shops, 19 February 1909

24 A bill to consolidate, amend, and extend the Shops Regulation Acts 1892 to 1904, 4 August 1909—Parliamentary Debates 1909, vol VIII, 19 July-6 August, 1849-54, 1698

25 19th Annual Report of the National Union of Shop-Assistants (1909), 2-3

26 Parliamentary Debates 1910, vol XIV, 354

27 Parliamentary Debates 1910, vol XVIII, 1339, 1340; vol XX, 235

28 *The Times*, 1910, 10 September, 16 September, 4

29 *The Times*, 14 September 1910, 8

30 Deputations received at the Home Office since the introduction of the 1910 Bill (Shops Bill) Cd. 5632, 1911, 15-20, 32, 148-51, 42-5, 46-9, 99-108, 114-25, 205-8

31 *The Times*, 14 November 1910, 8

32 Return of closing orders made by local authorities under Shop Hours Act 1904 between 15 August 1904-31 December 1910

33 Parliamentary Debates, vol XXII, 1911, 838, 1685-1746. Bill as passed by Standing Committee showing amendments to be proposed on Report, Cd. 5990. Parliamentary Debates, vol CCC, 1911, 680, 710; vol XXXII, 595-6

34 Hoffman, P. C. *They Also Serve*, 12

35 Parliamentary Debates, vol XXXII, 1786-1776-8

36 1 and 2 George 5, C.54

37 Gwynn, Stephen and Tuckwell, Gertrude M. *The Life of the Rt Hon Sir Charles W. Dilke, Bart, MP*, vol 2, 352

38 21st Report of the NUSA, 3

39 Public Record Office. H.O. 45/10687/226575

40 Public Record Office. H.O. 45/10687/226369

41 Ibid

42 22nd, 23rd, 24th Reports of the NUSA

43 Report of Departmental Committee on the Shops (Early Closing) Acts 1920 and 1921. Cmd. 3000, 1927, 5, 6, 7

44 10 and 11 George 5, C.58

45 11 and 12 George 5, C.60

46 Op cit, Ref 43, 9, 32, 34, 48, 59, 60, 62, 63, 11

47 18 and 19 George 5, C.33

48 24 and 25 George 5, C.42

49 14 George 6, C.28

Chapter 9

1 A Journeyman Engineer, *Some Habits and Customs of the Working Classes*, 1867, 201-2

2 Inquiries in the early 1950s showed that at that time no Early Closing Association records were known in the archives departments of the city of Bristol, the East Sussex County Council or the Kent County Council

Chapter 10

1 *Gravesend and Dartford Reporter*, 7 June 1879

2 Op cit, 1879, 14 June, 5 July, 2 August

3 Op cit, 1880, 3 January and 24 April

4 Op cit, 8 May 1880

5 Op cit, 22 May 1880

6 Op cit, 29 May 1880

7 Op cit, 17 July 1880

8 Op cit, 14 and 28 April 1880

9 Op cit, 19 May 1880

10 Op cit, 26 May 1880

11 Op cit, 2 June 1880

12 Op cit, 16 June 1880

13 Op cit, 29 September 1880

14 Op cit, 27 October 1880

15 Op cit, 24 November 1880

16 Op cit, 10 November and 17 November 1888

17 Op cit, 26 April, 28 June, 12 July, 8 November 1890

18 Op cit, 10 January 1891

19 Op cit, 21 January 1891

20 *Gravesend and Northfleet Standard*, 7 October 1892

21 *Gravesend and Dartford Reporter*, 24 March, 6 October, 10 November 1894

22 Op cit, 19 October 1895

23 Op cit, 18 January, 4 April, 18 April, 7 November 1896

24 Op cit, 6 November 1897

25 Op cit, 23 November, 21 December 1901

26 Op cit, 27 February 1904

27 Op cit, 15 October 1904

28 Op cit, 22 April 1905

29 Returns of Closing Orders 1904—31 December 1910. Cd.5499, 1911

30 Returns of Orders under Shops Act 1912 from 1 May 1912 to 30 April 1913. Cd.7032, 1913

Table of Hours in the Old Kent Road, London, submitted to the Select Committee by Mr D. C. Cornes on 7 April 1892. See also—with additional examples—Early Closing Association Report for 1891, p 16

Trade	No of Shops	Opening Hours	Closing Hours M.Tu.W.	Thursday	Friday	Sat night or Sun morning	Total Hours
Baker	24	7.30am	10pm	10pm	10.45/11.30pm	12.15/1.15am	91
Boot and Shoe	27	8/8.15	10	10 at 5, 17 at 10	10.15/11	11.45/12.30	80/87
Butcher	26	7.30/8	10	10	10.30/11.15	12.15/1.15	86/91
Cheesemonger, Provision Dealers	15	7.30/8	10	10, 1 at 5	10.30/11.45	12.15/1.15	86/92
China and Glass	2	8/8.45	10	1 at 10	10.30/11	12/12.30	80/87
Confectioner	20	7.30/8	10	17 at 2, 1 at 5, 4 at 10	10.30/11	12.15/1	86/91
Draper	22	8/8.45	9.30/10	3 at 5, 18 at 10	9.30/10.30	11.45/12.45	75/87
Grocer	22	8	9.30/10 (1 closes 5 on Mon)	1 at 5, 4 at 10	10.15/11	12/1.15	80/88
Ironmonger	6	7/8.30	10	3 at 2, 1 at 5, 4 at 10	10/10.30	11.15/12.15 (1 closes 5pm)	80/90
Milliner	8	8	10	3 at 2, 1 at 5, 4 at 10	9.30/10.30	11.45/12.45	80/87
Oil and Colour	16	8	10	10, 1 at 2, 4 at 9.30/10	10.15/11.15	12/12.45	86/88
Stationer	5	8/8.45	9.30/10	5	10/10.30	11.15/12.15	80/86
Tailor and Outfitter	10	8/9	9.30/10	1 at 5	9.30/10	11.15/12.15	75/81
Watchmaker	8	8/9	10	7 at 10	9.30/10	11.15/12	80/86

APPENDIX 2

Table of Shop Hours compiled from the Report from the Select Committee of the House of Lords on Early Closing of Shops, 1901

Place	Opening Hours	Closing Hours Mon.Tu Thur	Closing Hours Wed (or Thur)	Closing Hours Fri	Closing Hours Sat	Total Hours for Week
London, West End Better Class	—	6 or 7	6 or 7	6 or 7	2	—
London, Brixton, Peckham Better Class	—	7 or 8	2	7 or 8	8 or later	—
London, Brixton, Peckham Smaller Better Class	—	9.30 or 10	2	9.30 or 10	10 or later	—
London, General Smaller and Poorer	—	9	2 (usually)	10	11	—
London, General (Estimate of Union of Shop-Assistants)	—	—	—	—	—	75/80
London, Lambeth Walk	8 (bigger shops 9)	10.30	2	11	12.30	—
London, Lambeth Walk Greengrocers	8	10.30	10.30	11	12.30 and Sun 9/1	—
London, Walworth	—	9.30 or 10 but earlier Thur	9.30 or 10	12	12	—
London, Grocers in 368 Shops	—	—	—	—	Average 16 hrs on Sat	Average 79 a week
London, Drapers in 600 Shops	—	—	—	—	—	60/90: majority 72/76
London, Butchers						

Place	Opening Hours	Closing Hours Mon.Tu Thur	Closing Hours Wed (or Thur)	Closing Hours Fri	Closing Hours Sat	Total Hours for Week
London, Bakers 6,000/7,000 shops and 90 per cent work	—	10	10	10	12 or 12.30	90
Birmingham						
Drapers High Class	—				—	60/75
Drapers Poorer Class in Suburbs	—					75/90
West Bromwich		9	1	10	12	—
Plymouth						
General		7/8	2	7/8	9	—
Co-operative		M.Tu 6 Thur 7	1	9	9.30	—
Kingston-on-Thames	8	8	2	8	9.30 or 10	—
Huddersfield	8.30	8 or 9	8 or 9	8 or 9	8 or 9	—
Hull (Generally)	8.30	8	1	8	10 or 12	—
" (Side Strs.)		11	11	11	11 or 12	—
Portsmouth	8	8.30 or 9	(Not clear if any early closing) Close earlier but hours not given; presume 2	11 or 11.30	11 or 11.30	74/80
Nottingham						—
Middlesbrough						
Stockton-on-Tees, Thornaby 224 Shops employing 1,029 Assistants	8	7/9		11 or 11.30	11 or 11.30	
Average hours of these:						
11 Shops employing 156 Assistants						55 and under 60
48 Shops employing 304 Assistants						60 and under 65
130 Shops employing 494 Assistants						65 and under 70

Place	Opening Hours	Closing Hours Mon. Tu Thur	Closing Hours Wed (or Thur)	Closing Hours Fri	Closing Hours Sat	Total Hours for Week
16 Shops employing 36 Assistants	—	—	—	—	—	70 and under 75
19 Shops employing 39 Assistants	—	—	—	—	—	75 plus
Yorkshire, West Riding	8	8	8	9	10.30 or 11	—
Leeds, Hairdressers	—	—	—	9	11	72/87
Wolverhampton, Grocers	8	8	2	—	—	—
Bradford, Grocers	8	7, 7.30 or 8	7, 7.30 or 8	10	10 or 11.30	—
Accrington, Grocers	7	(8–8 2 days; 8–9.30 2 days; 8–11 or 11.30 one day; 8–1 Wed)				70
Bristol, Grocers	—	—	—	—	—	—
Better- and Middle-Class Trade	—	—	—	—	—	80/90
Working-Class Area	—	—	—	—	—	66/90
Liverpool, Grocers	—	Mon Wed Thu } 7	Tu 1	—	—	—
Co-op	8	—	—	9	9	—
Butchers	—	—	—	—	—	80 (if Sunday trade 85/87
Fruiterers	—	—	—	—	—	62/92 (longer if Sunday opening)
Oldham, Grocers	—	—	—	—	—	75/85: some 90
Co-op	—	8	Half-day	9	6	—
Jarrow-on-Tyne, Co-op	—	—	—	—	—	Longest hours 65

Census taken by National Amalgamated Union of Shop-Assistants
Outside London. 198 Middle-Class Shops showed

495	Assistants	worked	48	hours	but	under	60	hours
1,030	„	„	60	„	„	„	65	„
1,841	„	„	65	„	„	„	70	„
2,068	„	„	70	„	„	„	75	„
132	„	„	75	„	„	„	85	„
2	„	„	85	plus				

BIBLIOGRAPHY

Books

Ablett, William. *A Few Every Day Hints addressed to the Youths and Young Men of the Drapery Trade*, 2nd ed, 1856
Adburgham, Alison. *Shops and Shopping*, 1964
Anderson, Will. *The Counter Exposed*, 1896
Anonymous. *Business Life. The Experiences of a London Tradesman*, 1861
  Handy Book of Shopkeeping, 1866
  Hints for Country Shopkeepers, 1847
  Practical Testimonies of the Benefits attending the Early Payment of Wages, 1858
  Rules of the Metropolitan Drapers' Association, 1845
  Saturday Half-Holidays and the Earlier Payment of Wages—Speeches, 1856
  Shop Life and its Reform, Fabian Tract no 80, 1897
  The Shopkeeper's Guide, 1853
Armstrong, H. B. J. *A Norfolk Diary* (extracts, 1850-88), 1949
Arthur, William. *The People's Day—An Appeal to the Right Hon Lord Stanley*, 1885
  The Successful Merchant, 1852
Black, Clementine. *Sweated Industry and the Minimum Wage*, 1907
Blatchford, Robert. *Dismal England*, 1899
Bondfield, Margaret. *A Life's Work*, 1948
Booth, Charles. *Life and Labour of the People in London*, vol VII, 1896; final volume, 1902
Brassey, Thomas. *Work and Wages*, 1872
Brockway, Fenner. *Socialism over Sixty Years, the Life of Jowett of Bradford*, 1946
Bready, J. Wesley. *Lord Shaftesbury and Social-Industrial Progress*, 1933
Briggs, Asa. *The Age of Improvement*, 1959
Cadbury, Edward. *Women's Work and Wages*, 1906
Clark, G. Kitson. *The Making of Victorian England*, 1962
Cumming, John. *Lecture on Labour, Rest and Recreation*, 1856

P

Davies, Thomas. *Prize Essay on Evils . . . produced by Late Hours of Business*, 1843

Davis, Harry J. (and Smeeton, W.). *The Necessity of Early Closing to Self-Culture*, 1855

Dennis, John. *The Pioneer of Progress*, 1860

Duff, Hon Mrs Adrian Grant. *The Life Work of Lord Avebury, 1834-1913*, 1924

Escott, T. H. S. *England : Its People, Polity and Pursuits*, 1885

Fitzgerald, John. *Duty of Procuring More Rest for the Labouring Classes*, 1856

Flower, Edward. *Hours of Business*, 1843

Fulford, Roger. *Glyn's 1753-1935*, 1953

Graves, Charles L. *Mr Punch's History of Modern England*, vol 1, 1921

Greig, Mrs David. *My Life and Times* (printed for private circulation), 1940

Greville, Lady Violet. *Faiths and Fashions*, 1880

Grindrod, R. B. *The Wrongs of our Youth*, 1843

Hallsworth, J. *Protective Legislation for Shop and Office Employees*, 3rd edn, 1939

    (and Davies, R. J.). *The Working Life of Shop-Assistants*, 1910

Hammond, J. L. and B. *The Age of the Chartists*, 1930

Hayward, Arthur L. *The Days of Dickens*, 1926

Hobsbawm, E. J. *Industry and Empire*, 1969

Hoffman, P. C. *They Also Serve*, 1949

Hollingshead, John. *Ways of Life*, 1861

Hutchinson, Horace G. *Life of Sir John Lubbock, Lord Avebury*, 2 vols, 1914

Jefferys, James B. *Retail Trading in Britain, 1850-1950*, 1954

Jevons, W. Stanley. *The State in Relation to Labour*, 1882

Johnson, William. *England As It Is*, 1851

Journeyman Engineer (Thomas Wright). *Some Habits and Customs of the Working Classes*, 1867

King, A. J. *The System of Late Hours in Business*, 1843

Knight, C. B. *A History of the City of York*, 1944

Knox, John. *Signs of the Times*, 1855

Landels, Wm (Rev). *English Slavery and Early Closing*, 1856

Latimer, John. *The Annals of Bristol in the Nineteenth Century*, 1887

Layman (Wm Rivington). *The Late Payment of Weekly Wages*, 1854

Lectures. Delivered before the Young Men's Christian Association, 1845-6, vol 1, 1864

    'Seven on the Sabbath', 1852

Lilwall, John. *The Half-Holiday Question*, 1856

Martindale, Hilda. *From One Generation to Another, 1839-1944*, 1944

Mayhew, H. *Shops and Companies of London*, 1865

Miller, James. *Labour Lightened not Lost*, 1856

Page, Wm. *Commerce and Industry*, 1919

Philanthropos. *The Linen Drapers' Magna Carta*, 1839

Public Tribute. To Mr John Lilwall, 1858

Ralph, James (Rev). *Oppressive Shop Labour*, 1851

Rowe, Richard. *Picked up in the Streets*, 1880

Shipton, W. E. See Lectures

'Shop-Assistant'. *Behind the Counter*, 1888

Smee, Wm Ray. *National Holidays*, 1871
Smeeton, Wm. See Davis, H. J.
Smith, Albert, *Sketches of London Life and Character*, 1859
Sutherst, Thomas. *Death and Disease behind the Counter*, 1884
  Shop Hours Regulations—Correspondence, 1885
Taylor, J. R. *Government, Legal and General Saturday Half-Holiday* (report of Public Meeting, 1855), 1857
'Ten Years' Subscriber'. Remarks on Last Address of the Committee of the Metropolitan Drapers' Association, 1855
Tuckwell, Gertrude M. *The Life of the Rt Hon Sir Charles W. Dilke, Bt MP*, 2 vols, 1917
Vincent, Henry. *Early Closing Movement*, 1847
Wallace, Thomas (Rev). *British Slavery and the Duty of Abolishing the Late Hour System*, 1850
Webb, Sidney. *Labour in the Longest Reign, 1837-97*, Fabian Tract no 75, 1899
Webb, S. and B. *History of Trade Unionism*, 1907
Willcock, H. D. (ed). *Browns and Chester*, 1947
Wright, Thomas. See 'Journeyman Engineer'
Wynter, Andrew. *Our Social Bees*, 1861

Parliamentary Debates: Volumes of Hansard

1873 vol, March-May; 1884, April-May; 1886, January-March; 1892, February-March; 1893, vol X; 1895, vol XXX; 1896, vol XXXVII, vol XLIII; 1899, vol LXIX; 1901, vol LXXXIX; 1902, vol CIII; 1903, vol CXVIII; 1907, vol CLXX, vol CLXXIII; 1908, vol CLXXXVII; 1909, vol VIII, July-August; vol IX, August; 1910, vol XIV, February-March; vol XX, November; 1911, vol XXII, March; vol XXV, May; vol XXVI, May-June; vol XXVII, June-July; vol XXVIII, July; vol XXIX, July-August; vol XXX, October-November; vol XXXII, November-December

Parliamentary Reports

1855 Minutes of Evidence taken before the Select Committee appointed to consider the Expediency or Inexpediency of the Regulations contained in the Needlewomen, Limitation of Hours of Labour Bill (HL)

1875 Reports of the Inspectors of Factories for Half Year ending 30 April 1875

1886 Report from the Select Committee on Shop Hours' Regulation Bill

1892 Report from the Select Committee on the Shop Hours' Bill

1895 Report from the Select Committee on Shops (Early Closing) Bill

1901 Report from the Select Committee of the House of Lords on Early Closing of Shops

1908-9 Report of the Truck Committee, vol I-IV, col 442, 1908; 4443, 1908; 4444, 1908; 4568, 1909

1927 Report of Departmental Committee on the Shops (Early Closing) Acts 1920 and 1921. Cmd 3000, 1927

Other Reports

1844   The Third Annual Report of the Liverpool Association of Assistant
        Tradesmen
1844   The Fourth Annual Report of the Liverpool Association of Assistant
        Tradesmen
1844   The Late Hours System—Full Report of Speeches at a Meeting of
        the Drapers' Association
1844   Late Hours of Business among Shopkeepers—Report of a Public
        Meeting at Liverpool, 10 April 1844
1847   A Verbatim Report of the Fifth Annual Meeting of the Metro-
        politan Early Closing Association
1848   Report of Sixth Annual Meeting of the Metropolitan Early Closing
        Association
1889-94 Reports of the Early Closing Association
1892-1914 Annual Reports of the National Union of Shop-Assistants

Other Parliamentary Papers

Home Office—Deputations received since Introduction of 1910 Bill (Shops
    Bill), Cd 5632 (1911)
Return of Closing Orders under Shop Hours' Act (1909)
Return of Closing Orders 1904-31, December 1910, Cd 5499 (1911)
Return of Orders under Shops' Act 1912 from 1 May 1912 to 30 April 1913,
    Cd 7032 (1913)
Public Record Office—H.O. 45/10687/226369 and 226575

Bills

1884   Factory Acts (Extension to Shops) Bill
        Bill ... brought in by Sir John Lubbock
        Bill to Regulate the Hours ... in Shops ... in the City of Liverpool
1886   Bill to Limit the Hours ... of Children and Young Persons in Shops
        Bill to Regulate the Hours of Labour in Shops
1887   Bill to provide for the Earlier Closing of Shops
1889   Shops (Weekly Half-Holiday) Bill
1890   Shops (Weekly Half-Holiday) Bill
        Bill to Amend the Law relating to the employment of Women and
        Young Persons in Shops
        Bill to give Salaried Shop-Assistants one Half-Holiday in each week
        without closing the Shop
1892   Bill to Amend the Law relating to the employment of Women and
        Young Persons in Shops
        Shops (Weekly Half-Holiday) Bill
1893   Bill to Amend the Shop Hours' Act, 1892
1896   Bill to Amend the Law relating to Shops
        Bill to provide that all Shop-Assistants shall have one Half-Holiday
        in each week

Bill for Earlier Closing of Shops
1901 Bill to Amend the Law relating to Shops
1903 Bill to Amend the Law relating to Shops
(Early Closing) (House of Lords)
1904 Bill to provide for the Early Closing of Shops
Bill to amend the Law relating to Shops
1907 Bill to Amend the Law relating to Shops
1909 Bill to Amend the Law relating to Shops
Bill to Consolidate, Amend and Extend the Shops' Regulation Acts,
1892-1904
Bill to provide for the Closing of Shops and the Prohibition of Street
Trading on Sunday
1911 Shops' Bill

Acts

1886 49 & 50 Vict. C.55. An Act to Limit the Hours of Children and
Young Persons in Shops
1888 51 & 52 Vict. C.38. Renewed the above
1892 55 & 56 Vict. C.62. An Act to Amend the Law relating to the
Employment of Young Persons in Shops
1893 57 & 57 Vict. C.67. An Act to Amend the Shop Hours' Act of 1892
1895 58 Vict. C.5. An Act to Amend the Shop Hours' Act of 1892
1899 62 & 63 Vict. C.21. An Act to provide for Seats being supplied for the
use of Shop-Assistants
1904 4 Edw. 7. C.31. An Act to provide for the Early Closing of Shops
1911 1 & 2 George 5. C.54. Shops' Act 1911
1920 10 & 11 George 5. C.58
1921 11 & 12 George 5. C.60
1928 18 & 19 George 5. C.33
1934 24 & 25 George 5. C.42
1950 14 George 6. C.28

Newspapers and Magazines

Annual Register, 1843, 1871, 1888, 1900, 1902, 1903, 1904, 1906, 1907, 1911
Capital and Labour, 1874-8
Chambers' Journal, 1864
Daily Chronicle, 1898
Draper, 1869
Draper and Clothier, 1859-62
Early Closing Advocate, 1854
Evangelical Magazine, 1845, 1855
Fortnightly Review, 1895
Gravesend and Dartford Reporter, 1879, 1880, 1883, 1888, 1890, 1891, 1894,
1895, 1896, 1897, 1901, 1904, 1905, 1907
Gravesend and Northfleet Standard, 1892
History Today, April 1951, December 1971

Illustrated London News, 1848, 1871, 1882
Labour Light and Local Trades Unions' Journal, 1890
Lancet, 1851
Leader, no 2, 1890
Liverpool Monthly, 1838
London Quarterly and Holborn Review, 1949
Punch, 1860, 1861, 1886
Shop-Assistant, 1896
Shopkeeper, 1908-9
Shopkeeper and Assistant, 1899
Shop Life Reform, 1891
Social Science Review, 1864
The Times, various years from 1825 to 1911
Tomorrow, 1896
Warehouseman and Drapers' Trade Journal, 1891
Wesleyan-Methodist Magazine, 1863, 1873
York Herald, 1854
Yorkshire Gazette, 1854, 1902
Yorkshireman, 1854

Books of Reference

Grocers' Year Book, ed J. A. Rees, 1926
Minutes of the Wesleyan Methodist Conference in Birmingham, 1844

ACKNOWLEDGEMENTS

I have had an interest in, and been gathering material for, this book for more than twenty years. Many of those who made possible my searches for material, in various libraries and other places, no longer hold the offices they then did and I apologise to those whose help I may now have forgotten. Some are no longer alive.

No work of this nature is possible without making use of the resources of the Library of the British Museum in London and at Colindale. Over many years, going back long before my work on this subject, I have been indebted to the unfailing courtesy and helpfulness of many anonymous officials of the library. Some books, difficult or impossible to trace there, I found through the kindness of the Librarian, Mr J. H. P. Pafford, MA and his staff in the Goldsmiths' Library of the University of London. I have used the Public Record Office, the York Reference Library, the Central Reference Library of the City of Bristol, and received every assistance from those responsible for dealing with my inquiries.

The editor at the time of the *Gravesend and Dartford Reporter* gave me facilities to go through the files of the paper in the Gravesend office.

The research officer of the Union of Shop, Distributive and Allied Workers at Dilke House, London, made it possible for me to examine material there.

I hope that I have acknowledged in the References and Bibliography all those upon whose work I have drawn. If I have omitted any I sincerely apologise for the oversight.

I thank Mrs A. Payne of Hooe for her care and interest in the exacting job of typing the final draft of the book.

Above all, my thanks are due to my wife. But for her continued interest in its progress, patience in reading and re-reading many drafts, and her valued suggestions, this book would never have been completed. She has been willing to forgo many hours which we should have spent together so that I might become immersed in books and papers connected with what has been for me a fascinating hobby.

Finally, the sole responsibility for faults of omission or commission is mine and should in no way be attributed to any of those who have given me help.

WILFRED B. WHITAKER

Bexhill-on-Sea

INDEX

THIS BOOK TO BE RETURNED BY: